Get Connected for College

The Savvy Student's Guide to

College Prep

Beverly Gillen

D1509708

Get Connected for College: The Savvy Student's Guide to College Prep

Front and Back Cover Photos:
Gustavus Adolphus College – Tom Roster
Students – istockphoto.com
Author Bio – Kyle Krohn
Creek – John Sammler
Campus Photos – John Gillen

Publishing Consultant: Charlene Torkelson
Cover and Logo Design: Julie Lindstrom Design

ISBN-13: 978-1499202427

ISBN-10: 1499202423

Note: The information in this book is intended to be a reference for those seeking college preparatory guidance. The content is accurate and credible to the best of our knowledge but not meant to replace the advice of a physician, mental health provider or other professional. If legal advice or other assistance is required, a professional should be consulted. The information is intended as a helpful resource but offered with no guarantee of results on the part of the author. The author disclaims all liability in connection with the use of this book.

To my husband John
for his unwavering support and encouragement

To my daughters Molly and Megan
for being my guinea pigs as I learned about college prep

To my childhood family
for installing a love of reading and cheering me on

This book is also dedicated to today's students
who are tomorrow's leaders

Contents

Gustavus Adolphus College

1

The College Prep Dilemma:
(A Note to Parents)

"An investment in knowledge pays the best interest."
~ B. Franklin

Preparing for college admission can be an overwhelming process but you're not alone. *Get Connected for College* was written as a resource just for you—busy students and their even busier parents who want the inside scoop on planning for college. Perhaps you've already been wondering when to start looking at schools or take the first ACT/SAT test. Perhaps you've been meaning to teach your child about personal finance or simply show them how to do their own laundry. Many families are just trying to keep up with the demands of daily life and haven't had a spare minute to research life skills or college admission timelines. While sending a child off to college is the hope and dream of many parents, navigating the process can be a daunting task.

Consider these stats:

- Admission rates showing percent of applicants admitted in 2014: Carleton College (25.6%), Boston College (28.8%), Washington University in St. Louis (17.9%), University of California Los Angeles (22%). (1)
- Nationally, the average student to counselor ratio is 473-1. According to the American School Counselor Association, Minnesota ranks as having one of the worst ratios in the nation with only one counselor for every 771 students. (2)
- Average annual total charges for a private nonprofit four year college in 2013-14 were $40,917. (3)
- As of 2012, 71% of college seniors graduated with an average of $29,400 of student loan debt. (4)

(1) US News and World Report Rankings and Reviews Best Colleges
http://colleges.usnews.rankingsandreviews.com/best-colleges
(2) Sources: U.S. Department of Education, National Center for Education Statistics, May 2012, American School Counselor Association
(3) College Board's Trends in College Pricing 2013
(4) www.projectonstudentdebt.org

The admission stakes are clearly high. With college costs increasing, college admission becoming more competitive, and student debt hitting record levels, it is more important than ever to be well prepared and informed. As a parent educator and business professional, I was surprised to find myself quite unprepared for the challenge of coaching my first child on the intricacies of college prep and Life Skills 101. While schools generally do a good job preparing students academically, most do not have the resources to hand hold families through the admissions process or spend valuable classroom time on nonacademic subjects. Parents are often caught off guard that their child has not acquired all the competencies and leadership experiences that are essential for a successful transition to college. As I networked with other moms and dads, I discovered my husband and I were not the only ones struggling to find answers—other families were too.

Out of frustration, I decided to research the college prep topic myself. I visited campuses to speak with admission counselors and current college students. I analyzed college admission report data and created a list of recommended resources. Finally, I interviewed college planning professionals and subject experts. *Get Connected for College* is the end result of this research. The book is intentionally written to appeal to students using a youth friendly format with a *what's in it for me* mentality.

Parents will also benefit by using the book as a handy resource that connects all the college prep pieces together. Instead of spending sleepless nights worrying that you missed an important milestone, readers of *Get Connected for College* can relax and enjoy the college prep journey! Discover valuable tools including:

- Top 100 College Competencies® across 10 subject areas
- Over 250 practical *Make it Happen* ideas
- *Get Connected* college prep resources
- 4C's of Connection

- *My Milestone Map* with checklists for grades 6 - 12
- Campus Collection tip sheets including Spotlight on Scholarships, College Scorecard, 25 Ways to Make a Difference, 25 Ways to Start Saving for College and more!

Meet Our Subject Experts

Students and parents need reliable information, and it can be difficult to determine who and what is a trustworthy source on the Internet. *Get Connected for College* has team of experts to ensure that credibility. These professionals have reviewed the College Competencies® and/or college prep milestones so families can be assured they are accessing accurate information.

Whitney Frisch, Educator, Certified Career and Life Coach

Whitney Frisch is an accomplished and knowledgeable educator and school administrator with over 20 years of experience in providing quality educational experiences for children and adults. She has a Master of Science Degree in Curriculum and Instruction from Minnesota State University and a Bachelor of Science in Elementary Education from the University of Wisconsin. Whitney is also a Certified Career and Life Coach specializing in individualized career planning services.

Dr. Angela Busch, MD, Ph.D.

Dr. Angela Thompson-Busch is a pediatric hematologist-oncologist in Grand Rapids, Michigan. She received her medical degree from Johns Hopkins University School of Medicine in 1995 after completing a Ph.D. in pharmacology at the University of Michigan in 1991. She is board-certified in pediatrics and has special interests in hematology/oncology, adolescent gynecology, and ADHD/autism.

Dr. Gerry Foo, LP, Ph.D.

Dr. Gerry Foo is a licensed psychologist with a Ph.D. in clinical and developmental psychology from the Institute of Child Development, University of Minnesota. In his practice, Psychological Solutions for Children and Adolescents, he provides cognitive behavior therapy for individuals and families. His primary areas of expertise include the assessment and treatment of anxiety and depression related to stress in high-achieving individuals.

Linda Keene, CEO of the Girl Scouts of Minnesota and Wisconsin River Valleys

Linda Keene provides vision and leadership to one of the largest Girl Scout councils in the nation, serving more than 40,000 girls. Ms. Keene holds an MBA from Harvard University Graduate School of Business Administration and a BA from Boston University School of Management, from which she received the Distinguished Alumni Award in May 1999.

Jim Gilbert, Consulting Naturalist

Jim Gilbert is a consulting naturalist for WCCO Radio, coauthor of the Minnesota Weatherguide Environment Calendar, author of four books and writer of the Minneapolis Star Tribune nature column. Jim previously served as Director of the Minnesota Landscape Arboretum and taught the Environmental Studies Program at Gustavus Adolphus College.

Um! Yah! Yah!

Congratulations Graduates!

2

Get Connected for College

"It takes a village to raise a child."
~ Old African proverb

College life is exciting! It is your chance to live independently, choose a major, and make lifelong friends. Perhaps you are dreaming of the day you arrive on campus, or maybe you have some reservations about this major life transition. The process itself can be a bit overwhelming, but you don't have to go it alone. From colleges to corporate workplaces to community organizations and caring adults, there are lots of people in your community who want to see you succeed. Whether you are in middle school or a senior in high school, it's never too late to *Get Connected for College!*

Connect with Caring Adults (CA)

Teens enjoy spending time with their friends but when it comes to college prep advice, consider asking a trusted adult. Moms, dads, aunties, grandpas, guidance counselors, neighbors, clergy, or teachers are good places to start. Here are some suggestions on how to initiate the conversation:

- Ask your CA about their experience. Did they go to college? Why or why not? What would they do differently if they were a student today?
- Ask your CA for feedback on your college admission essay.
- Help your CA do something you want to learn like cooking or checking your tire pressure.

Connect with Colleges

Middle school is the perfect time to start exploring colleges:

- Do some research to discover which colleges are in your state. Residents receive a discount on public colleges or universities, so local schools are a good place to start your search.
- Most colleges have informative websites where you can find stats including tuition rates, number of students, majors and activities.
- If you have an older sibling or a relative in college, ask if you can visit for the day. Seeing the campus firsthand helps you evaluate if the culture is a good fit for you.

- Attend a college sponsored summer camp. Camps allow you to meet a coach or music director from that school and see what it is like to live in the dorms.

High school is the time to deepen connections with colleges:
- Take advantage of your high school's college visit days where you can meet college reps.
- Attend a college sporting event, rally or concert.
- Schedule an appointment/tour with the admissions office.
- Ask about the option to visit overnight and observe a class.

Connect with Community Organizations

Look around your community and you'll find organizations that exist solely for the purpose of doing good works. Boy Scouts, United Way, and faith communities are just a few examples of nonprofits that focus on *making a difference*. Taking time to meet your community neighbors can benefit you in several ways:

- Resource and referral—know where to go if you or a friend needs help.
- Volunteer experience—develop new skills you can add to your resume.
- Leadership opportunities—take charge and show colleges what you're made of.

If you're not sure where to start, we've included a list of *Get Connected* resources at the end of each chapter.

Connect with Corporations

Smart companies are investing in youth as they realize today's teens will be tomorrow's workforce. Businesses are devoting time and money to support programs including scholarships, mentoring, and school STEM initiatives (science, technology, engineering, math). You can usually find out what opportunities a company might offer by viewing the company's website or by calling their Human Resources department:

- Part-time jobs—explore a work setting while you're earning cash for college.
- College scholarships—odds of winning a local scholarship are much greater than entering a national competition.
- Internships—although typically unpaid, you gain valuable experience and connections.
- Mentoring—opportunities vary by company and may include: E-mentoring, mock interviewing, tutoring, robotics coaching, science fair judging, and summer camp advisors.

Campus Tour Time

University of St. Thomas

3

Take the Quiz

"Anyone who stops learning is old, whether at 20 or 80."
~ Henry Ford

Are you ready for college? Do you know how to do your own laundry? Balance a checkbook? Schedule your own doctor appointment? Did you know there are 100 College Competencies® that will help you be more successful in college? Students today are busier than ever before and without intentional effort, it is easy to graduate without having the critical skills needed to survive dorm life. Invest in your independence by mastering the Top 100 College Competencies® and you will be confident on campus in no time.

Start by taking the quiz to assess your College Competency IQ (Independence Quotient) and then have fun exploring the ten subject areas:

1. America the Beautiful
2. Eco Adventure
3. Get Around Town
4. Health and Happiness
5. Household (Help!)
6. Show Me the Money
7. Social Scene
8. Sports and Fitness
9. Technology
10. World of Work

The College Competencies® model was created as a tool students can use to develop knowledge in practical matters beyond academics. Each topic has *Make It Happen* suggestions and *Get Connected* resources. AND, we've partnered with subject experts to bring you credible and up to date information.

Go to our website www.partnersinparentingconsulting.com and Take the Quiz. Once you have your results, go after the skills you want to develop (each competency is numbered for your handy reference.) Pick a subject area that interests you or one you don't know much about, and check out the *Make It Happen* ideas. Take your time and have fun learning more about topics and you'll be prepared for campus life in no time!

*Please note while Take the Quiz is a thought provoking exercise, it is not a scientific study, behavioral analysis or psychological evaluation. Results are simply intended to highlight subject areas you may enjoy learning more about.

Girl Scout Gold Awardees

4

America the Beautiful

"Never doubt that a small group of thoughtful, committed citizens can change the world. Indeed, it is the only thing that ever has."
~ Margaret Mead

We all have the ability to give back, so don't let the opportunity pass you by. You can get involved in your community in lots of ways, by voting or taking time to thank a veteran, or singing along to the National Anthem. In just a few years, today's 13 - 18 year olds will be the leaders of tomorrow. That's you! There are six civic-related competencies to help you become an active, engaged citizen of your community.

#1: Volunteer

Helping others without expecting anything in return is a great way to learn new skills and meet new people. This experience is valuable when it comes time to apply for college, as most colleges want to recruit students who are active in their community. Students who complete an extensive volunteer project might be eligible for special scholarships.

Make It Happen

➢ Schools, places of worship, or scouting programs are great sources of volunteer opportunities. Offer to help with a small project to see what interests you and expand from there.

➢ Keep a log of your community service activities. Note the date, organization name, supervisor and number of hours so you can recall this information later when applying for National Honor Society, college, and scholarships.

➢ High school students are eligible to join National Honor Society with a qualifying GPA and forty hours of community service. Applications are generally taken during the junior year of high school.

#2: Vote

Casting your vote on an issue is empowering and a way you can personally make a difference in your community. Instead of complaining that something's not fair, take action. Knowing how to state your opinion in a professional and persuasive manner is a powerful tool to influencing others. Smart corporations and lawmakers will be listening to the opinions of our nation's teens who are the next generation of decision makers.

Make It Happen

➤ Cast your vote at school. Many schools have programs to tally student ballots for national elections or encourage them to choose their student council representatives.

➤ Try voting at home. Encourage the democratic spirit by voting on where to spend the next family vacation or other fun issue. Get involved by researching the issue, costs, pros and cons and presenting your case to your family board of directors.

➤ Contact your local government official. Is there something in your community that isn't fair or could be improved? Send an email or letter stating your case in a positive, professional tone and offer several ideas on how you think the issue can be solved. Be sure to include your contact information so the official can send you a response back.

➤ Are you a senior in high school who has turned 18? Register to vote and don't miss out on your first chance to choose a president or participate in a local election.

#3: Recite the Pledge of Allegiance

You may remember growing up saying the Pledge of Allegiance in school. Although most high schools don't say the Pledge daily, it is also used at important ceremonies and civic occasions. Participate with pride by remembering the words to this statement about freedom and love for your country.

Make It Happen

➤ Reacquaint yourself with the Pledge words and etiquette. It is proper to stand during the Pledge, take your hat off, and place your hand over your heart.

➤ If your religion does not allow the word God, substitute or skip this part. Find the words that work for you that allow you to honor your country.

#4: Sing the National Anthem

The Star-Spangled Banner is a well known patriotic song that was written by Francis Scott Key and was named America's National Anthem in 1931. Sports fans know that most games are preceded by the singing of the National Anthem. Those that know the words look more confident and are great role models to younger citizens.

Make It Happen

➤ Learn about the history of this song and why we sing it.

➤ Sing in the shower. If you never learned all the words to the song, print them out and post them up somewhere you will see them regularly.

➤ Go to a game. Take your new found skill and enjoy belting out the words at a baseball or football game or figure skating competition. It is proper etiquette to stand during the song, take off your hat and place your right hand over your heart.

➤ Contact local sports teams and ask if students can lead the crowd in singing the anthem before a game. Encourage them to print the words in the program so the crowd can sing along.

#5: Know Your Rights

Do you know your rights? Think beyond the rules at your house to your rights at school, your job, your state, another country. American law grants many freedoms that are easy to take for granted. Protect yourself by brushing up on your human rights history.

Make It Happen

➢ The Bill of Rights is a symbol of American freedom. Because of this amendment to the Constitution, Americans have free speech, the right to a public trial, and the freedom to practice a religion of their own choice. Learn more about all ten amendments and the people who fought for our rights at http://kids.usa.gov/teens.

➢ Be an advocate for yourself and others. Know that youth have special rights under the United Nations Convention on Rights of the Child (CRC). This document has been signed by every country in the world and gives kids the right to an education, freedom of expression, safe working conditions and more. See how UNICEF helps make a difference at www.unicef.org.

➢ Know the laws in your city and state. Browse your city's website for rules that apply to teens like curfew times and driving restrictions. If you are planning a spring break trip, be sure to read up on the laws of that country.

#6: Contact a Government Official

Want to change the world or just fix something that annoys you? Knowing who to contact and how to phrase your complaint or suggestion in a persuasive manner is important if you want people in power to take you seriously.

Make It Happen

- ➢ Address your issue with the appropriate official. For example, although the President of the United States has a lot of power, your local mayor would be the better person to address a concern over city curfew times.

- ➢ Contact the official by phone, email or letter. State your concern in a respectful manner and list any suggestions you have for solving the problem. Thank them for their consideration and include your contact information so they can follow up with a response.

- ➢ Make an appointment to meet with an official in person. Be prepared to greet the official with a business handshake, and follow up the meeting with a thank you note.

Get Connected Resources

Boy Scouts of America www.scouting.org

Boy Scouts prepares young people to be responsible, participating citizens and leaders as guided by the Scout Oath and Law.

Doing Good Together www.doinggoodtogether.org

As a national nonprofit, Doing Good Together's aim is to make family volunteering accessible, easy, and enjoyable. The site has project ideas and resources for raising generous, civic-minded children.

Do Something www.dosomething.org

Do Something's aims to inspire, empower and celebrate a generation doers: young people who recognize the need to do something, believe in their ability to get it done, and take action.

Girl Scouts of the USA www.girlscouts.org

The Girl Scout organization is dedicated solely to girls, where girls build skills for success in the real world. Girl Scouting builds girls of courage, confidence, and character, who make the world a better place.

MN State Legislature Links for Youth www.leg.state.mn.us

Website has a special page for young adults with info spotlighting recent laws, who represents me, homework helpers, how a bill becomes a law.

National Honor Society www.nhs.us

NHS serves to honor those students who have demonstrated excellence in the areas of scholarship, leadership, service, and character. Site has information on membership criteria, scholarships and chapter finder.

National Mentoring Partnership www.mentoring.org

MENTOR's mission is to fuel the quality and quantity of mentoring relationships for America's young people and to ensure that every kid who wants a mentor has one.

United Way www.unitedway.org

United Way's mission is to improve lives by mobilizing the caring power of communities around the world to advance the common good.

YMCA www.ymca.org

YMCA's mission is to build strong kids, strong families, and strong communities. YMCA offers youth development programs including Black Achievers, sports, camps and Youth and Government.

Rake-a-Thon

Stuck in the Mud, AP Environmental Science Class

5

Eco Adventure

"One generation plants the trees; another gets the shade."
~ Chinese Proverb

Whether you live in the country or a suburb or the city, you can make a difference in the environment. Your generation will eventually inherit the Earth, so there's no time to waste. Have you visited a local state park this year? Are you using energy efficient light bulbs at home? Do you use a re-usable water bottle instead of a disposable one? There are eight environmental competencies that teach students how to enjoy and respect the earth.

#7: Reduce

R3 = reduce, reuse, recycle. Media tries to convince consumers we can't go without the latest trendy products, but think for yourself and consider your impact on the environment. If you limit the number of purchases you make, you will have less to reuse or recycle later on.

Make It Happen

➢ Reducing what you consume is simple and is as easy as turning off the lights (energy), taking the bus or carpooling (gas), shortening your shower (water), or buying your favorite item in a less bulky package (garbage). Have a contest with your friends or family to see who can implement the most energy saving ideas.

➢ Replace your old incandescent bulbs with the most energy efficient technology. Check the Energy Star website for proper disposal of your old bulbs.

➢ Plastic water bottles are a huge source of waste. Invest in a BPA free bottle that can be used over and over again and save around $200 per year. Put the extra money in a vacation fund or donate to your favorite eco cause.

➢ Support your local co-op grocery store. They carry many items in bulk so you only have to buy the quantity you need and skip the bulky packaging. Bring a reusable shopping bag to tote your new goods home.

#8: Reuse

Before tossing something in the garbage, ask yourself if it can be used again or for a different purpose. While some disposable items are convenient, reusing items cuts down on waste and has come back into fashion as an eco friendly option. Consider buying a higher quality item that lasts longer to extend your purchasing dollars.

Make It Happen

➢ Celebrate your graduation in style with reusable party ware and decorations. Skip messy food that requires plastic forks and choose finger food like mini burgers or hotdogs. Instead of buying hundreds of plastic cups, fill a decorative pitcher with water, ice and slices of fresh fruit and serve in paper cups. Decorate using flowers that can be planted after the party.

➢ There is a wise old saying that *one man's trash is another man's treasure.* Clean out your closets and host a garage sale for your neighborhood. Invite some friends to help and post some fliers in the community to advertise your sale. It's fun to bargain and an easy way to earn some spending money.

➢ If you don't have time to organize a yard sale, consignment shops are a great option! Some stores specialize in clothes while others sell home goods. Bring in your jeans or that old bike and the store will either pay you cash on the spot or log your items and pay you when they sell.

#9: Recycle

Almost all cities now have recycling programs that collect household cans, plastics, newspapers and other items. Encourage your family to do their part and keep America beautiful!

Make It Happen

➢ Recycling at home is easy and most cities provide curbside pickup. Call your garbage service and ask them for a better rate on a smaller size trash can. Many cities now offer organics recycling which further reduces the amount of trash. Set aside the money saved for a special occasion.

➢ Organize a recycling collection for charity. The Lions refurbish and donate old eye glasses and donate to those who can't afford to buy them. Collect pop can tabs for the Ronald McDonald House to help kids with cancer. Collect pop cans and bring them to a metal retailer for cash, then donate the money to your favorite cause.

➢ Electronics change at the speed of lightning but what happens to all the old phones and computers and accessories? Many of these products have components that should not be thrown in the trash so contact your county to find out how to safely dispose of these items. Demonstrating responsible behavior might work in your favor the next time you are asking your parents for the latest device.

#10: Leave No Trace

Have a favorite beach or park or vacation area? Practice the seven principles of leave no trace and you can enjoy the outdoors while reducing your impact. Planning ahead, disposing of waste, and respecting wildlife are just a few things you can do to support this philosophy. Feel good about protecting the environment, and ensure your favorite place is healthy for years to come.

Make It Happen

- ➤ Taking a hike is great exercise and a way to work off stress. Hike on an established trail and leave rocks, flowers and other natural objects as you find them.
- ➤ Plan a campout adventure at one of the state parks. Check to see if fires are permitted and if so, keep your fire small and use a fire ring. When finished, put out your campfire completely and scatter the ashes. Inspect your campsite for garbage before you leave.

#11: Navigate

Finding your way in the woods can be extremely challenging without some navigational tools. Learn how to navigate your way using low and high tech methods and you will be ready to tackle any outdoor adventure.

Make It Happen

- ➤ Practice using a map and compass before venturing into the woods. The compass needle always points to magnetic north. The base card has four quadrants that tell you which direction you should go to head south, east and west. Try navigating around a local park or neighborhood with a friend.

➤ A Global Positioning System (GPS) is a practical tool for finding your way in the outdoors. Simply enter the coordinates for your destination before you head out on the trail and follow the easy to read instructions.

➤ Challenge yourself and learn how to navigate the old fashioned way in case technology fails. The sun is in the east in the morning, in a southerly direction at midday, and in the west in the evening. Tie brightly colored items to trees as you pass and note any major landmarks.

➤ Tell someone where you are going and what time you'll be home. Even a veteran hiker can lose their way or have a medical emergency and need rescuing so it pays to have someone else know your approximate whereabouts.

#12: Weather Watch

Red skies at night, sailor's delight. Red sky at morning, sailors take warning; is an old but true saying that people used to help them predict the weather. Tornados, snowstorms, and heat waves can cause the unprepared traveler lots of headaches. Don't get caught out in the storm by brushing up on your weather safety tips.

Make It Happen

➤ Find out how your city alerts its citizens of severe summer weather. Many cities have sirens that sound if a tornado has been sighted nearby or broadcast warnings via television and radio. Unfortunately, many storms hit at night when people are sound asleep. Visit your local electronics store and price out a weather radio.

➢ If you live in a cold climate, assemble a winter storm kit for your car: scraper, sand, candy or granola bars, water, candle/matches, red bandana, blankets and an extra set of clothes. If riding with friends, heed mom's advice and bring your mittens and hat in case you get stranded.

➢ Take care of yourself on a hot summer day by getting plenty of water and wearing sunscreen. Bring a water bottle to the beach or purchase a sports drink with added electrolytes. Be familiar with the signs of heat stroke or heat exhaustion so you can help a friend if needed.

#13: Grow a Garden

You don't need a lot of space or time to try your hand at gardening. Growing your own food is fun and an inexpensive way to get fresh produce that hasn't been treated with chemicals. The Food Guide Pyramid recommends eating more than five servings of fruit and vegetables each day so start now by planting one of your favorites.

Make It Happen

➢ Try planting a container garden. Any plant that can be grown in a full size plot can be grown in a container, just match the container size to the size of your plant. Tomatoes, corn and beans are especially easy to grow!

- ➢ Plant a theme garden. Choose peppers, garlic, tomatoes and onions to harvest the ingredients for your own custom salsa.
- ➢ Talk to your family about buying produce from a Community Supported Agriculture (CSA) farm. CSA members pay a small fee and in exchange, receive a share of locally grown produce during the growing season. Many CSA farmers use little or no chemicals and the food is very fresh, right from the field to the fork.

#14: Hang Out (side)

Don't wait for vacation to enjoy the outdoors. Biking, walking, going to the beach, reading at the park, and playing sports are all great ways to get outside. Trade some screen time for green time, and you can feel stronger, have better concentration and feel happier and more relaxed.

Make It Happen

- ➢ Do a reality check and log the number of hours you spend outside for one week. Next, challenge yourself to double the time you spend outdoors. Instead of playing video games after school, grab a friend or your favorite pet and take a walk. Try doing your homework outside. If you meet your goal, reward yourself with something fun you can do in the great outdoors.
- ➢ Plan a visit to a state or national park. Amaze yourself with nature's beauty whether it's a prairie, waterfall, forest, or lake. Take your camera and document your adventure.

> ➢ Live in a cold climate? Don't let a little snow and cold keep put you into hibernation. Test out the saying there is no such thing as bad weather, only bad clothing. Bundle up and go sledding or take shorter, but more frequent walks. The fresh air is a natural way to restore your concentration after a long day at school.

Get Connected Resources

Do It Green www.doitgreen.org

The main goal of the Do It Green! Minnesota is to promote sustainability with tips on energy, environment, health and more.

Lions Clubs International www.lionsclubs.org

Donate glasses and change someone's life by helping a child read or a senior to maintain their independence.

Minnesota Landscape Arboretum www.arboretum.umn.edu

The Arboretum features more than 1,000 acres of magnificent gardens, model landscapes, and natural areas. Tour the Arboretum on 12.5 miles of garden paths and hiking trails. Walk the close gardens and bike, walk or drive Three-Mile Drive.

National Gardening Association www.garden.org

NGA supports KidsGardening.org, a provider of grants and free materials for educators and families so that they may use gardening as a resource for learning.

National Wildlife Federation www.nwf.org

NWF is America's largest conservation organization. NWF works with communities across the country to protect and restore wildlife habitat and confront global warming.

Rethink Recycling www.rethinkrecycling.com

A go to guide for waste and recycling in the Twin Cities, an outreach campaign by the Solid Waste Management Coordinating Board of Minnesota.

The Freecycle Network www.freecycle.org

This network is a grassroots, nonprofit movement of people who are giving (and getting) stuff for free in their own towns.

Three Rivers Park District www.threeriversparks.org

Three Rivers Park District is a park system in the west suburban Minneapolis/St. Paul metro area of Minnesota. With facilities for every season, Three Rivers Parks is the place for recreation, play and relaxation.

Celebrating Winter at Luther College

6

Get Around Town

"Never drive faster than your guardian angel can fly."
~ Author Unknown

If you didn't have an older sibling or parent to teach you car care, it's not too late! Many technical colleges offer courses or you can focus on learning the basics like checking tire pressure or filling up the washer fluid. However you get around town, be sure to brush up on these travel tips. There are eight transportation competencies for newly mobile teens including tips on driving safely, car care, buying a car, and accessing public transportation.

#15: Drive a Car

Learning to drive is a rite of passage in the United States. After years of being chauffeured by others, it's a great feeling to jump in the car and drive yourself to school or a friend's house. Take this responsibility seriously to keep your new privilege and enjoy your independence.

Make It Happen

➢ Enroll in a driver's training course. You will receive instruction on the rules of the road and safety and then complete a test to get your learner's permit. Most courses also include behind the wheel training.

➢ Practice. A new driver lacks reaction skills and the ability to anticipate dangerous situations. With a patient adult, practice driving on different types of roads and weather conditions. Log as many practice hours as you can and you will ace the driving test!

➢ Be safe. Get used to good safety habits right from the start like turning off your cell phone (no texting!) and limiting the number of passengers in your car. Wear your seat belt and observe speed limits.

➢ Don't drink and drive. This seems obvious yet thousands of youth are killed in drunk driving accidents each year. Read and sign the Contract For Life agreement that is sponsored by Students Against Destructive Decisions (SADD).

#16: Fill up with Gas

Running out of gas is no fun so take time to learn how to fill up your tank. Although each pump is a little different, the basic operation is the same.

Make It Happen

➢ Ask an adult to show you how the pump works and then give it a try. Most pumps will prompt you through the process. You will need to know what type of fuel your car takes, if you prefer to pay inside/outside and with cash/credit.

➢ Fuel safely. Take your wallet or purse with you if you pay inside and lock your car doors. Don't allow a passenger to have an open flame near the pump as this could cause an explosion. Remember to close your gas cap before you leave.

#17: Check Tire Pressure

Car tires occasionally leak air and need to be refilled. You don't have to be a mechanic to check your own tires and fill them up. One of the best ways to get a smoother ride and better gas mileage is to make sure your tires are properly inflated.

Make It Happen

➢ Borrow a tire gauge and ask an adult how it works. Find the recommended pressure for your car in your auto manual or on the driver's side door jamb. Check all four tires and add air if needed. Recheck the pressure using your tire gauge.

➢ Live in a cooler climate? Don't get caught off guard with flat tires in the first cold snap. Because the cooler temps lower your tire pressure, it's important to reset the pressure in the fall, ideally in the morning when your tires are cold. Follow up with monthly checks after that.

#18: Fill Up Windshield Fluid

Most cars have a safety light that comes on when your car is low on washer fluid. Running out of fluid can actually be a safety hazard so take charge by learning how to perform this basic maintenance on your own.

Make It Happen

➢ Ask an adult to show you where the washer fluid reservoir is located inside your hood. Prop up the hood securely and unscrew the fluid cap. Add fluid and re-close. Keep fluid bottles out of the reach of small children and pets.

#19: Access Public Transportation

Taxis, trains and buses are common in big cities and are a great way to see the sights. New modes like light rail are becoming popular choices because they conserve fuel. Depending on where you live, using public transportation might be easier than driving a car.

Make It Happen

➢ Program your local cab company's number into your cell phone so you have it handy. Taxis are the most expensive option but are convenient if you need a quick ride to the airport or a ride home in an emergency. In a large city, you may be able to call a cab right off the street. Establish the fare up front. It is customary to tip a cab driver 15% of the fare.

➤ Look up your city's bus routes and pick up times on the Internet, and ask an adult for permission to take a trial run for fun. If you live in the suburbs, take a bus downtown and go shopping or to a sports event. If you live downtown, take a bus to an outlying suburb and have lunch. Be prepared to pay your fare when you get on the bus. If you need to get off before the last stop, pull the hanging cord or press the button to alert the driver to stop. Tips are not required.

#20: Find Your Way

Some people have the gift of navigation and can find their way anywhere without a map. If you are not one of those people, use a tool like MapQuest or a Global Positioning System (GPS) so you arrive at your destination on time.

Make It Happen

➤ Internet sites like Mapquest allow you to plug in your starting and ending addresses and produce step by step directions on how to get to your destination. Practice trying to find a location close to home and then check out the advanced features for longer trips.

➤ Experiment using a Global Positioning System (GPS). Instead of printing your directions ahead of time, your GPS is portable and uses a satellite to find the best route. Enter your starting and ending addresses and the program will produce a map and the road names along the route to help you reach your destination.

#21: Drunk Driver Safety

Drunk drivers tragically kill thousands of people each year. Driver impact panels tell heartbreaking stories of people that have killed someone accidentally and wish they could turn back time. Don't become a statistic and take these precautions when you are a passenger or behind the wheel.

Make It Happen

➢ Don't drink and drive or get in a car with someone who has been drinking. Alcohol slows down your response time which is critical to operating a vehicle. Make an agreement with your family that if you ever need a ride, they will pick you up, no questions asked that evening.

➢ Stay off the roads after midnight. You are far more likely to encounter a drunk driver after midnight. If you are attending an event that ends after midnight, consider asking an adult to pick you up.

#22: Buy a Car

Buying your first car is exciting! Arm yourself with research and negotiation techniques to get the best deal for your money.

Make It Happen

➢ Consider buying a used car. As soon as it's driven off the lot, a brand new car's value takes a big drop. You can save thousands of dollars and still get a great car by driving something a few years older. Sites like Carsoup.com help connect buyers and sellers.

➢ Find out how much a specific model should cost by using Internet sites like KBB.com and Edmunds.com. Plug in the year, make, mileage and features and these sites will give you ballpark figures you can use to negotiate with the seller.

➢ Know what to expect from a car dealership, and bring an adult along for support. Talk in terms of the invoice price the dealer paid (no markup) and come prepared with printouts from an Internet site that document this information. Test drive the vehicle and if it's a used car, consider having a professional mechanic examine the car for problems. You are purchasing a commodity, so don't be afraid to shop around for the best price.

Get Connected Resources

Distraction.gov www.distraction.gov

A U.S. Department of Transportation resource for learning more about distracted driving. Get the facts, pledge forms, videos and way to get involved to keep America's roadways safe.

Metro Transit www.metrotransit.org

Metro Transit is the transportation resource for the Twin Cities, offering an integrated network of buses and trains as well as resources for those who carpool, vanpool, walk or bike.

Minnesota Department of Public Safety www.dps.state.mn.us

The Vehicle and Services division offers valuable resources including drivers education schools, road test checklist, teen driver contract, and traffic laws for teen drivers.

Students Against Destructive Decisions www.sadd.org

A peer-to-peer education, prevention, and activism organization dedicated to preventing destructive decisions, particularly underage drinking, other drug use, risky and impaired driving, teen violence, and teen suicide.

Tire Rack Street Survival School www.streetsurvival.org

Use your own car to learn about its handling limits and how you can control them, providing teens with a *hands-on* driving experience in real-world situations.

511 Traveler Information www.511mn.org

A public service of the Minnesota Department of Transportation (MnDOT) with information about road conditions, traffic incidents, and weather information via the phone or the Web, twenty four hours a day, seven days a week.

Snowshoeing Sweethearts

7

Health and Happiness

"Every day brings a chance for you to draw in a breath,
kick off your shoes, and dance."
~ Oprah Winfrey

Taking care of your physical, mental and emotional self is a big job. Are you getting enough sleep each night while managing to get your homework done? Do you know the signs of depression and ways to de-stress when life gets too hectic? Do you have a game plan on how to resist drugs and alcohol? Chapter 7 covers twelve wellness competencies that help teens take care of their minds and bodies.

#23: Perform CPR

Cardiopulmonary Resuscitation (CPR) is a life saving technique that combines a series of chest compressions and rescue breathing. You never know when you might be in a position to save a life so it's a good idea to take this training. Displaying this certification on your resume will give you an advantage in the summer job market, especially if you want to work as a lifeguard or in a child care setting.

Make It Happen

➢ Take a CPR class through your community education department or the American Red Cross. Spread the word and encourage a family member or friend to attend with you.

➢ Add your new certification to your resume, noting the date and name of the certifying organization.

#24: Perform Basic First Aid

Basic first aid teaches the responder to check the ABC's of the victim (airway, breathing, circulation) and to provide care until professional help arrives. Feel confident that you could help yourself or others in an emergency. This certification is also good to list on your resume.

Make It Happen

➢ Know how to call 911. Dialing the number is easy but remembering to stay calm and speak clearly takes some focus. If dialing from a cell phone, the dispatcher won't automatically know your location so you need to tell him what city you are calling from and the type of emergency.

➢ Take a first aid class through your community education department or the American Red Cross and encourage a family member or friend to attend with you. Add your new certification to your resume.

➢ Assemble a first aid kit for your car. Band-Aids, latex gloves, a breathing barrier and nonstick pads are good items to keep on hand.

#25: Manage Your Medication

Taking charge of your own medication is a step to independence. Keeping track of the prescriptions you take, the reason you take them, when to take them and how to refill them is important to keep yourself healthy.

Make It Happen

➢ Read up on any medication you plan to take so you understand what the benefits and risks are and any side effects it may have. If you have questions, your local pharmacist is a good resource.

➢ With your parent's permission, start managing the dosage and timing of your medication. It may be helpful to write down the time you took your medicine on a family calendar.

➢ Call in your own prescription and pick it up at the pharmacy. For refills, the pharmacist typically needs the prescription number, name of the patient, and insurance information. For new prescriptions, your doctor needs to call in the prescription ahead of time or you can bring the hard copy order to the pharmacy.

#26: Get a Good Night's Sleep

Have a hard time getting up in the morning? Teenage brains need 8.5 - 9.5 hours of sleep to perform well in sports and school, be alert at the wheel, and get along with family and friends. Make sleep a priority to stay healthy and be ready to do your best.

Make It Happen

➤ Analyze your schedule. Are you trying to fit too much into one night? Cutting back on even one activity might be the trick to getting to bed on time.

➤ Avoid caffeine, exercise, computer and TV an hour before bed. Do homework earlier in the evening to avoid a last minute rush. Enjoy calm, quiet activities later in the evening and you should be able to fall asleep easier.

➤ Set an alarm on a clock radio or cell phone to wake yourself up in the morning. If you have trouble hearing the alarm, ask a family member to give you a wakeup call.

#27: Self Defense

Personal safety goes beyond *stranger danger*. Keep yourself safe by traveling in a group and anticipating unsafe settings.

Make It Happen

- ➤ Go with a group. You are less likely to be targeted for a crime if you are with a group of people. Bring your dog instead of walking alone. Even tiny terriers can bark and snap threateningly to discourage a potential attacker.

- ➤ Communicate your plans. Let someone know where you are going and what time you expect to be home.

- ➤ Trust your intuition. If you get that worrisome feeling, don't blow it off or worry about not being polite. Heed your body's warning signals and go to a safe place instead.

- ➤ Take a self defense class. Learn some simple moves that could help you get out of a dangerous situation. If confronted, use your voice to yell words like fire, police, or help to call attention to your situation.

#28: Eat Healthy

Mom was right if she told you to eat your veggies. The Food Guide Pyramid recommends eating more than five servings of fruits and vegetables each day. Fuel your body with food rich in vitamins and protein and you will have more energy and look and feel great!

Make It Happen

- ➤ Instead of eating ice cream after school, try making a smoothie. Combine frozen fruit, a banana, and milk or yogurt in a blender and puree for a delicious treat that is packed with vitamins but low on calories.

➤ Breakfast is the most important meal of the day but it can be hard to fit in when you're rushing to school. Don't miss out! Grab one of these quick options: yogurt and fruit, hardboiled egg, frozen waffle with peanut butter.

➤ Visit a natural food co-op. Organic food is a super healthy choice because the produce has not been grown with any chemicals or pesticides. Ask the manager which foods are on the Dirty Dozen list and buy the organic version.

#29: Stress Less

Tests, speeches, sports competitions, bosses, family conflicts, and arguments with friends are all common sources of stress. While a little stress can actually be motivating, stress overload takes a toll on your body. Find a stress buster that works for you and you'll feel more calm and optimistic in no time.

Make It Happen

➤ Practice relaxing. Take time out of your busy schedule to read a good book, take a warm bath, do relaxation breathing, or take a walk in nature.

➤ Attend a yoga class. Yoga is mind calming and great for enhancing your flexibility.

➤ If your stress is making you sad or anxious, consider visiting with counselor or therapist. They are good listeners and are trained to help you find solutions to your problems.

#30: Prevent Illness

Getting a day off from school is fun but not if it's because you're home sick with a cold or the stomach flu. Help keep yourself germ free by washing your hands, not sharing drinks with friends, and getting enough sleep.

Make It Happen

➤ Washing your hands the right way is one of the best things you can do to keep well. Use soap and warm water and then lather up while you sing the ABC song in your head. Rinse off and use a clean towel to dry your hands. If you are in a public restroom, use a paper towel to open the door on your way out. Keep a small bottle of hand sanitizer in your purse or backpack.

➤ Check your vaccine record to make sure you are current on immunizations. While no one likes to get a shot, they protect you from many diseases like whooping cough and tetanus. Several new vaccines have become available in the last few years so give your doctor a call to make sure you're covered.

#31: Prevent Pregnancy

Abstinence means to *refrain deliberately* and is the only way to prevent pregnancy 100%. Having sex is a big decision and one that could result in premature parenthood. Babies are sweet but are incredibly expensive and caring for them requires all your extra free time. Knowing how to protect yourself can save you from shopping in the diaper aisle any time soon.

Make It Happen

➢ Make sure you know the facts behind the *birds and the bees* story. If you haven't had this conversation, consider asking a trusted adult or health teacher for the facts.

➢ Take time to make a good decision. Are you feeling pressured by your partner or peers? How does it fit with your values? Could you afford to postpone your education and care for a baby 24 hours a day? Consider talking to a trusted adult for advice.

➢ If you decide not to abstain, take proactive measures to protect yourself and your partner from pregnancy or disease. Visit a teen clinic to have an exam and obtain condoms and other birth control. These clinics specialize in working with youth and are a confidential resource for health counseling.

#32: Substance Smarts

Smoking, alcohol and drugs are unfortunately common in schools and neighborhoods. Know your facts about these substances so you won't get tricked into trying them. Students who remain chemically free do better in school and have healthier, stronger bodies.

Make It Happen

➢ Get the word out about the tobacco industry. Tobacco companies would go out of business if they couldn't convince any more youth to start smoking. Research has proven that smoking causes cancer but tobacco companies continue to market their products to youth regardless of health concerns. Smoking is also very expensive. Better to skip the cigarettes and use the money for a nice vacation instead!

➢ Never drink and drive or get in a car with someone who has been drinking. As a family, read and adopt the principles in SADD's Contract for Life, a document that encourages youth and adults to communicate about issues related to alcohol, drugs and peer pressure.

➢ Choose your friends wisely. Positive peers support each other in making good choices. They find alternate ways to have fun like attending sporting events, dance parties, or bonfires.

#33: Recognize Depression

It's normal to feel sad sometimes, but when this feeling doesn't go away, it could be clinical depression. Many people experience depression at some point in their life. By knowing the symptoms of depression, you could help yourself or a friend in need.

Make It Happen

➤ Familiarize yourself with the signs of depression. They include: feelings of hopelessness, loss of interest in daily activities, loss of appetite, and sleep changes.

➤ Ask for help. The key to feeling better is letting others know what you're going through. Contact your doctor or a mental health counselor for professional guidance.

➤ Educate yourself on suicide prevention. If someone you know is threatening suicide or saying they want to hurt themselves, seek out professional help immediately.

Get Connected Resources

Al-Anon/Alateen www.al-anon.alateen.org

Al-Anon/Alateen is a support group for family members and friends of alcoholics. Call: (888) 4AL-ANON.

American Red Cross www.redcross.org

The American Red Cross offers international disaster relief, community services that help the needy, support for military families, the distribution of lifesaving blood and educational programs that promote health and safety.

Bridge for Runaway Youth www.bridgeforyouth.org

The Bridge for Youth in Minneapolis offers individual and family counseling to help families before they reach the breaking point. Services include: 24-hour hotline, walk-in counseling, family counseling, emergency shelter, transitional living program.

Choose My Plate www.choosemyplate.gov/MyPlateOnCampus

A site sponsored by the US Department of Agriculture with tips on healthy eating, MyPlate on Campus Toolkit, recipes and resources.

Emily Program www.emilyprogram.com

This program provides a personalized approach to eating disorders treatment and helps individuals challenge and change thoughts and behaviors that prevent them from having a positive relationship with food, their bodies and themselves.

Kinship of Greater Minneapolis www.gmcc.org

Kinship is a mentoring program that encourages couples, families as well as individuals to spend quality time with boys and girls ages 5 to 18.

Let's Move www.letsmove.gov

Let's Move! is a comprehensive initiative, launched by Michelle Obama, dedicated to solving the problem of obesity within a generation, so that children born today will grow up healthier and able to pursue their dreams. The website has lots of tips for healthy eating and increasing physical activity.

MyHealth www.myhealthmn.org

MyHealth offers professional, low cost medical, mental health and health education to teens 12-23 in Hennepin, Carver and Scott counties of Minnesota.

National Domestic Violence/Abuse Hotline www.ndvh.org

A nonprofit organization that provides crisis intervention, information and referral to victims or domestic violence, perpetrators, friends and family. Call: (800) 799-SAFE.

National Teen Dating Abuse Helpline www.loveisrespect.org

Information on dating abuse and trained advocates available 24/7 who can offer support. Call: (866)-331-9474.

National Youth Crisis Hotline

Organization provides counseling and referrals to local drug treatment centers, shelters, and counseling services. Responds to youth dealing with pregnancy, molestation, suicide, and child abuse. Call: (800) 442 HOPE.

Rape, Abuse & Incest National Network www.rainn.org

This nationwide partnership of more than 1,100 local rape treatment hotlines provides victims of sexual assault with free, confidential services around the clock. Call: (800) 656-HOPE.

Students Against Destructive Decisions www.sadd.org

A peer-to-peer education, prevention, and activism organization dedicated to preventing destructive decisions, particularly underage drinking, other drug use, risky and impaired driving, teen violence, and teen suicide.

Suicide Awareness Voices of Education (SAVE) www.save.org

SAVE offers information on suicide prevention.
Call: (800) SUICIDE.

Teens Alone www.teensalone.org

Teens Alone provide confidential and free counseling and crisis services to teens and parents in the western suburbs of Minneapolis.

TeensHealth www.kidshealth.org/teen

TeensHealth is part of the KidsHealth family of websites. These sites, run by the nonprofit Nemours Center for Children's Health Media, provide accurate, up-to-date health information that's free of *doctor speak*.

TobaccoFree.org www.tobaccofree.org

Smokefree America's mission is to motivate youth to stay tobacco free, and to empower smokers to quit. Site includes links to anti-smoking resources.

United States Department of Agriculture www.mypyramid.gov

This website contains dietary guidelines using my pyramid model, interactive tools, and resources on food choices and weight management.

Exchange Student and Host Sisters

Making pizzas for Children in the Garden

8

Household (Help!)

"There's no place like home."
~ Dorothy Gale, The Wizard of Oz

How would you rate your household skills? Can you whip up a basic batch of mac and cheese and run a vacuum? Do you know how to sew on a missing button or remove ketchup from your new shirt? Start practicing these skills now and you will be a college roommate in demand. There are nine practical living skills that students should master before moving into a dorm.

#34: Do Laundry

Ever heard the story of the college student who saves up her laundry until Thanksgiving and brings it home for mom or dad to wash? Have fresh clothes whenever you need them by learning how to do your own laundry.

Make It Happen

➤ Ask an adult to show you how to operate your washing machine and dryer. Most models have just a few settings to choose from so it's really quite easy. Put in a practice load and you're on your way to laundry independence.

➤ Refine your laundry techniques. Wash similar colors together to avoid fading or bleeding. Use detergent that is concentrated and formulated for cold water to save energy. Fold clothes as soon as they are dry to prevent wrinkles.

#35: Plan a Meal

Outside of cooking class, have you ever planned an entire meal before? A healthy meal includes some type of protein, vegetable or fruit, a starch, and beverage. While fast food is convenient, preparing a meal with fresh ingredients from your own kitchen is healthier and less expensive.

Make It Happen

➤ Surprise your family and offer to make dinner. Plan your courses and make note of special ingredients you may need to shop for ahead of time. Making dinner two to three nights a week might be a good way to increase your allowance.

➤ Organize a progressive dinner party for friends. The party starts at one house for appetizers and then moves to the next house for the salad course. Another friend hosts the main course, and then the party travels to the last house for dessert.

➤ Learn new recipes and stock up on dinners at one of the *make and bake* businesses around town. Have fun cooking in a professional kitchen and go home with several ready-made meals that can be frozen and used on busy school nights.

#36: Cook a Simple Dish

There's something comforting about the smell of fresh baked cookies or a pot of soup on the stove. Learn to cook and you can make your favorites whenever you like. Homemade dishes are usually more economical and healthier too!

Make It Happen

➤ Look online or in your family's favorite cookbook to find recipes you'd like to make. Keep it simple to start. Casseroles, soups, and muffins are usually pretty easy.

➤ Watch a cooking show on TV. Besides being entertaining, the chefs have good tips and recipe ideas.

➤ Turn on the oven and start cooking! This is a fun activity to do with friends, especially around the holidays. Make several batches of cookies and donate some to a senior citizen in your neighborhood.

#37: Clean a House

While cleaning might not be your favorite chore, it is a necessary evil. Dusting, vacuuming, scouring the bathroom and washing the kitchen floor are part of maintaining a household. Using these skills now will help you be prepared to maintain your own home someday.

Make It Happen

➢ Shock your family and ask for a lesson in how to clean a particular room. While they are still in shock, offer to do this chore on a regular basis and perhaps you can earn extra allowance money.

➢ Look online for earth friendly cleaning solutions. Vinegar and water works well for cleaning glass, and baking soda is a good all purpose solution.

➢ Start your own cleaning business. Families are so busy today that they might be interested in hiring a teen to help tidy up. Being an entrepreneur is great experience for your resume not to mention a good source of cash.

#38: Wash Dishes

Washing your dirty dishes is an everyday task that needs to be done. Most dishes can be washed in a dishwasher but it's good to know how to scrub them the old fashioned way. Larger pots and pans and delicate items like crystal will need individual attention.

Make It Happen

➤ Learn how to operate a dishwasher. Stack plates and bowls so they face the water spray and make sure to use soap that is formulated for a dish washer (not dish detergent) or you could end up with bubbles all over your kitchen.

➤ Choose a night when you have lots of dirty pots and pans from dinner and help out by washing a load by hand. Fill the sink half full with hot water and add dish detergent. Use a nylon scrubber for tough spots, and then rinse your dishes with hot water so they dry faster. Sponges attract bacteria so either change them very frequently or use a dish cloth that can be sanitized.

#39: Mow a Lawn

In some families, kids are expected to mow the lawn. If your chore list does not include mowing or you don't have a lawn, you can still learn this skill for the future. Mowing is good exercise and a decent paying summer job for students.

Make It Happen

➤ Ask an adult to show you how to operate the mower. Check to make sure it has gas and the grass height is set correctly. Wear close-toed shoes to protect your feet and noise blocking headphones to protect your hearing.

➤ Start your own mowing business. Offer something your competitors don't, like free doggy doo pick up before each mowing. Consider using a rotary mower that does not use gas and is better for the environment.

#40: Hang a Picture

Have a new poster you'd like to hang up in your room? You don't have to be a certified builder to perform this task. Arm yourself with a few tips and a hammer and you can take charge of your own decor.

Make It Happen

➤ Check with your family to make sure they approve of the location for your new piece of art. Heavy pictures are best positioned over a wall stud for stability. The center of the picture should be equal with the height of adult eyes.

➤ Ask an adult to demonstrate the proper technique. You will need a hammer, nail, wire hanger and tape measure.

#41: Care for a Child

Taking care of a small child is one of life's most rewarding but challenging jobs. Kids need different care at different ages and no two kids are exactly alike. Babysitting is a nice way to earn money and develop your skills as a leader.

Make It Happen

➤ Take a babysitting class to learn the basics of child development and safety. The American Red Cross offers this course and you earn a certification at the end of the session.

➤ Put your new skills into practice by babysitting for a family that lives nearby. Put your cell phone calls from friends on hold while working. Plan something special like a scavenger hunt to have the kids asking for you again and again.

#42: Sew a Button

Lost the button on one of your favorite shirts? Don't wait for grandma to visit to get this fixed. Sewing a button is a common repair that just takes some patience, a needle and thread.

Make It Happen

➢ Use thread that matches the color of your button. Thread your needle and tie a knot in one end. Place the button on the garment and bring the needle up from the wrong side of the fabric. Push the needle down into the opposite hole and continue this pattern until the button is sewn on tight.

Get Connected Resources

Energy Star www.energystar.gov

This program helps save money and protects the environment through energy efficient products and practices. Americans, with the help of ENERGY STAR, saved enough energy in 2010 alone to avoid greenhouse gas emissions equivalent to those from 33 million cars—all while saving nearly $18 billion on their utility bills.

Habitat for Humanity www.habitat.org

This organization develops communities with people in need by building and renovating houses. Volunteers can develop household maintenance skills while helping those in need.

Minnesota Parents Know www.mnparentsknow.info

This site is hosted by the Minnesota Department of Education and is provided for parents following extensive parent input and research. Trusted parenting information, resources, and activities to help your child grow, develop, and learn from birth to high school.

Yum-o! www.yum-o.org

Launched in 2006 by Rachael Ray, Yum-o! is a nonprofit organization that empowers kids and their families to develop healthy relationships with food and cooking by teaching families to cook, feeding hungry kids and funding cooking education and scholarships.

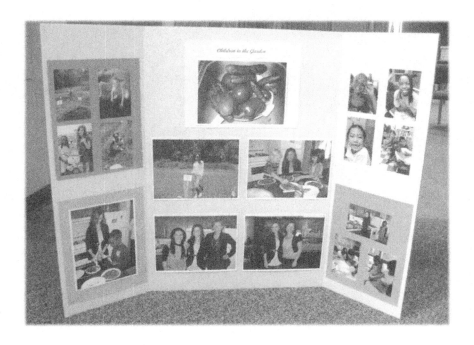

Children in the Garden Project

Your author learning her first business skills

9

Show Me the Money

"Happiness is not in the mere possession of money: it lies in the joy of achievement, in the thrill of creative effort."
~ *Franklin D. Roosevelt*

Have you always been intrigued by business and enjoy managing money? If this resonates with you, congratulations! If the prospect of going to the bank or negotiating a purchase sounds like torture, don't despair. This chapter is filled with tips on shopping, budgeting, managing credit, financing college, and investing, all you need to know to be successful in organizing your personal finances before you head off to college.

#43: Count Back Change

The ability to quickly and correctly calculate change has not gone obsolete with the invention of computerized cash registers. As many retail managers know, machines can fail, electricity can go out, but business must go on. A student that can perform this function with confidence will be a valued employee. This skill also comes in handy for personal shopping.

Make It Happen

➤ Practice at home. Ask a family member to purchase several items from you and add up the purchases in your head. Announce the total due, take their payment, and then count back their change starting with the coins. When you have handed over the last bill, remember to thank your customer.

➤ Take your new skill on the road and set up a bake sale, lemonade stand, car wash or other money making venture. Make sure to have coins and a variety of bills in your cash register so you can make the appropriate change.

➤ Put your new skill to work at a part-time job as a teller, sales clerk, or food server. Amaze your customers with your speed and smile!

#44: Purchase Something at a Store

It's empowering to make a purchase all by yourself for the first time. Purchasing goods and services can be a lot of fun (shopping!) but, as the Latin saying goes, *let the buyer beware.* Thrifty shoppers can save money if they pay attention to sales and ensure that they receive any advertised discounts.

Make It Happen

➢ Approach the sales counter and present your items to the sales clerk. If the items are on sale, make sure your final price reflects the discount. Some states charge sales tax which may add a small amount to the total you owe.

➢ Count your change. If you pay for your purchase with a bill larger than the total cost, you will receive change back. Be sure to count your change before leaving the sales counter and if you find a discrepancy, notify the sales clerk of the error. Save your receipt in a safe place in case you need to return the item later.

#45: Return Something at a Store

Returning an item is never as much fun as purchasing one. Sometimes an item has a defect, or perhaps you received a gift that really wasn't your size or style. Experienced shoppers will know how to successfully make an exchange and get their money back so it can be used for a better purpose.

Make It Happen

➢ Put the item you plan to return in its original bag or packaging if possible, along with the receipt and any tags. Present the return to the sales clerk along with the receipt. The clerk may ask the reason for the return and feel free to be honest about why you are bringing the item back. Without a receipt, the store may only offer a store gift card instead of cash back. It's a good habit to ask what the return policies are at the time you make the initial purchase.

#46: Make a Bank Deposit or Withdrawal

Stashing your allowance in a drawer may be convenient but is not the wisest place to keep your cash. Start a relationship with your local bank and you will have a safe place to keep your growing income. Depending on the type of account you choose, you may be able to earn extra money in the form of interest.

Make It Happen

➢ If you don't already have a savings account, ask your family if you can open one. Many banks offer special accounts just for students.

➢ Save up your allowance and then visit the bank to make a deposit. Fill out a deposit slip which states how much money you are depositing, the date, and your account. The teller will give you a receipt once the transaction has been completed.

➢ To take money out of your account, simply fill out a withdrawal slip. This form usually requires your signature so the bank has proof that you authorized a reduction from your account. The teller will give you a receipt along with your money once the transaction has been completed.

#47: Analyze a Savings Account Statement

It's fun to watch your savings grow. You can do this by depositing money on a regular basis and by reviewing your savings account statement. Banks can make mistakes so it's important to check the statement against your receipts to make sure all your transactions show up correctly.

Make It Happen

➢ Compare the ending balance from your last statement to the starting balance of your new statement to make sure the totals are the same. Check to see all your deposits and withdrawals are shown in the correct dollar amounts. Make note of your final balance and file your statement.

#48: Calculate a Gratuity

Leaving a gratuity (tip) is a way to express appreciation to someone who performs a service for you. Hairstylists, food servers, pizza deliverers, housekeepers, and manicurists are just some of the jobs that rely on tips for part of their income. Knowing when to tip and being able to quickly calculate the amount is an important skill for those that enjoy these services.

Make It Happen

➢ Decide whether a tip is appropriate. Is this service one that typically receives a gratuity? Sometimes the service wasn't the best and it may be tempting to leave no tip at all. Most people in service occupations really enjoy helping people but sometimes circumstances can be beyond their control. Think hard before stiffing someone. Generous, compassionate customers usually receive better service than critical ones.

➢ It is customary to leave 15-20% of the bill as a tip. If your bill was discounted for any reason, be sure to tip on the total amount before the discount was applied.

#49: Set Up a Budget

Budgeting is having a simple plan for saving, spending, and sharing your money. Without a plan, it's easy to spend your whole allowance on payday and then be penniless until your next check. Take a few minutes to create a budget, and you may end up with more money to spend in the end.

Make It Happen

➤ Make a plan. Add up your average *income* for one month. This may include allowance, gift money, or salary from a part-time job. Add up your average *expenses* for one month and separate them into three categories: Spending, Savings, Sharing. The total of your income should equal the total of your expenses.

➤ Keep track of your actual spending/savings/sharing patterns for two months and compare to your budget. It's easy for little purchases to add up to a lot of money without realizing it. Are there things you could buy less of that would allow you to save or share more? Make a list of simple changes you could make to save even more money.

#50: Negotiate

Have you heard the phrase *everything is negotiable?* You'd be surprised how many things you can negotiate a better a deal on just by asking. Most companies are hoping consumers are too busy or shy or uninformed to bargain, but surprise them by being a pleasant and assertive negotiator and you might end up saving a lot of money!

Make It Happen

➢ Before making your next major purchase, do some preparation. The key is to create leverage, like having competitive prices from other stores. Ask to speak to the manager and let him know that you'd really like to buy this item from his store, but you have a better price from a competitor. Would he be willing to beat the price by a modest percent? The worst he can say is no and he just might say yes. You never know unless you try.

➢ Make a list of other opportunities to negotiate and set a goal for how many dollars you think you can save in the next six months. Use the extra money to fund your college account or another worthy purpose.

#51: Protect Your Identity

Identity theft occurs when someone steals your personal identifying information to commit a crime. Many victims spend countless hours trying to restore their good name and credit record so take steps now to protect your personal information.

Make It Happen

➢ Memorize your social security number and do not carry the card in your purse or wallet. This number uniquely identifies you from birth. It is required on many government documents and is thus highly prized by identify thieves. You may need to provide this data to apply for a job or on federal financial aid applications but it should not be required on many other standard forms.

➤ Take simple precautions to protect your privacy. Position yourself at the ATM machine so bystanders aren't reading account numbers over your shoulder and be sure to take your receipt with you.

➤ Don't use your mailbox for outgoing bills that contain checks or cash. Pick up your mail as soon as possible or use a post office box. Review your bank and credit card statements for false charges. Don't put sensitive documents in the recycling without shredding first. Request a free credit report once a year.

#52: Donate to a Good Cause

Perhaps you give a weekly contribution to your church or have collected money for the animal shelter. Sharing our resources with a charitable organization feels good and helps benefit others in need. If you pay taxes, the money you donate can be deducted from the tax you owe the government at the end of the year.

Make It Happen

➤ Before you donate to an organization, make sure it's a reputable one. Keep a record of your contributions for your taxes.

➤ Think about what causes are important to you and what you could do to support them. Decorate an old can and use it to collect spare change or add a little bit of your allowance each week. You'll be surprised how quickly change accumulates. Visit the organization, and donate your money in person.

#53: Understand Taxes

There are many kinds of taxes but they all have one thing in common. You pay precious money to the government that you could have used for something else. Understanding when and why something is taxed can help you avoid paying out more money than you need to.

Make It Happen

➤ Planning to make a big purchase? Don't forget that you will likely pay tax on top of the initial product price. Regulations vary from state to state. For example, Minnesota is still a bargain for clothes because they are exempt from sales tax.

➤ Filing taxes at the end of the year doesn't have to be stressful. Hire an accountant to help you or purchase tax software and submit your forms online. Ask an adult who is familiar with taxes to review your calculations first.

#54: Be Careful With Credit

Having a credit card is convenient for vacations and emergencies. Using a credit card responsibly helps build up good credit history which is important later on if you need to apply for a loan. Unfortunately, many people get carried away with credit and charge more than they can afford. Credit card fees can be very expensive so protect yourself by understanding how these cards work and use them to your best advantage.

Make It Happen

➤ Talk with your family about their philosophy on using credit. Do not apply for any cards without an adult's permission first.

➤ Find a card that has a good reputation and use it to build up your credit history. Check the Consumer Reports website for the best cards for students. Some offer cash rebates and smaller credit limits that help prevent overspending. Be sure to read the fine print on late charges and other hidden fees.

➤ Many credit card companies allow you to pay a much lower minimum due each month. Although this sounds attractive, it really means that you will be making payments for a much longer time and paying extra money in interest charges. Get in the habit of paying off the entire balance or waiting to purchase the item until you have the cash in hand.

#55: Importance of Investing

Although it might be tempting to spend your cash on clothes or electronics, consider investing your money instead. Companies sell stocks to raise money. The goal of investing is to buy a stock, hold it for a time period, and then sell it for more than you paid for it. It's fun to research which company's stock you want to buy. If you invest when you are young, your money has a longer time to grow in value.

Make It Happen

➢ Give investing a try by purchasing one share of stock. Companies like OneShare.com sell single shares of stock in companies that have products that appeal to youth. Monitor your stock's performance using the daily paper or the Internet. The higher your risk, usually the higher your reward.

➢ Join an investing club or ask if your school participates in a stock market competition. Using play money, work together with your school team to choose a stock portfolio that you think can outperform the other teams.

➢ Start a 529 college savings account. 529's are investment plans that are designed to help you save money for college. You don't need much money to start an account and the interest you earn is not taxed if it is used to pay for qualifying college expenses.

#56 Manage a Checkbook

Writing checks is a convenient way to buy things without having to hold large sums of cash. Your check acts as a permission slip, allowing the bank to deduct money from your account to pay for your purchase.

Make It Happen

➢ Open a checking account at your community bank. Some banks have student rates and special deals if you maintain a higher balance. Ask about overdraft protection so you won't get charged a fee if you mistakenly write a check for more than your account balance.

➢ To write a check, fill in the date, name of the person or company the check is to, the amount and the signature line. Some stores do not take checks so it's a good idea to ask before writing one. Most stores will ask for identification before accepting your check.

➢ Balance your checkbook at the end of the month to ensure your transactions were properly recorded and to bring your balance up to date.

#57: Use a Debit Card

Using a debit card is a handy way to pay for purchases without using cash or writing a check. After presenting your card to the clerk and signing for the purchase, the amount is automatically deducted from your bank account. Debit cards offer the convenience of credit cards without the risk of charging too much.

Make It Happen

➢ Visit your bank and inquire about getting a debit card. Remember to record your purchases to keep track of your balance.

➢ Compare your monthly bank statement to your spending record to make sure there are no errors or false charges.

➢ Watch out for fees. If you accidently charge more than you have in your account, the bank can charge an overdraft fee.

Using an ATM outside your own bank's network may also result in convenience fees.

#58: Pay a Bill

Any time you buy something on credit, you will need to pay a bill later. Paying your bills on time is important to protect your credit rating so banks and stores will want to do business with you again in the future.

Make It Happen

➤ Write a check. Enclose the invoice along with your check when you mail it.

➤ Pay online. Set up an account online and you can view your account balance and pay bills automatically. It's quick and you save money on postage.

#59: Use an ATM

Automated Teller Machines (ATM's) are convenient to use when you need cash and the bank is closed. ATM machines are located in many public places including grocery stores, malls, and workplaces.

Make It Happen

➤ You can obtain an ATM card from your bank. Memorize your Personal Identification Number (PIN) which will allow you to access your account at the machine. Insert your card and enter your PIN, the type of account and the amount for withdrawal.

- ➢ Take safety precautions. Position yourself so that someone in line behind you cannot read your account or PIN numbers. Be sure to take your card and receipt with you when you are finished. Avoid withdrawing large sums of cash alone at night or in an unsafe part of town.

#60: Finance Your College Education

Thinking about paying for college can be overwhelming but fortunately there are many good financial aid programs and resources available. Starting to save money early is one of the most important strategies. Getting good grades and demonstrating leadership and community service experience may help you qualify for merit based scholarships.

Make It Happen

- ➢ Open a 529 college savings plan. Make a goal to deposit a percent of your weekly allowance or paycheck and you'll be surprised to see how fast your account grows. The interest you earn is tax free if used for qualified college expenses.

- ➢ Find opportunities to gain leadership and community service experience through scouting, places of worship, or school. Colleges tend to give more merit aid to students who have gone above and beyond in giving back to their community.

- ➢ Keep up your grades and plan ahead for ACT/SAT tests. Consider working with a private tutor on ACT/SAT study skills and test strategies. If you can increase your score by several points, you may qualify for additional financial aid.

➢ Fill out the Free Student Application for Federal Student Aid (FAFSA). All families should fill out the FAFSA, regardless of income. Colleges have many forms of aid including merit aid, scholarships, and loans. Don't cross a college off your list because of its initial sticker price. Many private colleges have healthy endowment funds and give generous scholarships.

➢ Search out independent scholarships. Check your high school website for a listing of scholarship opportunities and apply for as many as possible. Local scholarships are usually easier to attain than national ones. Watch out for scholarship scams. You should never have to pay a fee to apply. Follow the directions of each scholarship carefully and be sure to send in your application well before the deadline.

#61: Understand Insurance

Insurance isn't the most exciting topic for party conversation but you should know how the basic concept works. There are many kinds of insurance including life, medical, auto, and home. You can buy coverage from a local agent, and in exchange for a fee, the company will reimburse you for damages according to your specific policy.

Make It Happen

➢ Before you can drive a car, you must be covered under an auto insurance policy. Do some research on the Internet to find competitive quotes and then compare those quotes to your family's current insurance provider. Consider changing your deductible to save money or negotiate with the agent using a competitive quote. Many companies also offer discounts for good grades.

➤ Watch your speed and keep your driving record clean. Auto insurance is expensive for youth because they are viewed as a risk by the insurance providers. If you get in an accident or receive a speeding ticket, your rates increase dramatically. If your family cannot afford to pay more for coverage, you could be left unable to drive again until you can pay for your own insurance.

Get Connected Resources

BestPrep www.bestprep.org

BestPrep's mission is to best prepare Minnesota students with business, career and financial literacy skills through experiences that inspire success in work and life.

College Savings Plans Network www.collegesavings.org

The College Savings Plans Network is a national nonprofit association dedicated to making college more accessible and affordable for families. The website provides detailed information about 529 college savings plans and allows you to compare plans from around the country.

Federal Student Aid www.fafsa.ed.gov

Federal Student Aid is an office of the U.S. Department of Education and provides many valuable resources on paying for college including the FAFSA4caster.

Junior Achievement www.ja.org

JA Worldwide is the world's largest organization dedicated to educating students about workforce readiness, entrepreneurship and financial literacy through experiential, hands-on programs.

Money as You Grow www.moneyasyougrow.org

Developed by the President's Advisory Council, this site offers age-appropriate financial lessons with corresponding activities kids need to know as they grow.

Learning the Merengue in Social Dance Class

10

Social Scene

"Manners are a sensitive awareness of the feelings of others.
If you have that awareness, you have good manners,
no matter what fork you use."
~ Emily Post

Most teens (and adults) would go to great lengths to avoid being labeled socially awkward. What is it about some people that make them appear so confident and gracious? Learning a few of life's finer social skills can go a long way in enhancing your charm. Would you bet your allowance on which is the proper fork to use at a formal dinner? Can you write a formal thank you note or dance the Waltz? There are 15 competencies to help you be socially savvy.

#62: RSVP

The acronym RSVP comes from the French phrase "Repondez s'il vous plait" and means please respond. When you receive a written invitation, it is proper etiquette to reply back to the host letting her know if you can attend the event or not. Hosts need to know how many people to expect so they can plan enough food and beverages. Simple courtesies like replying are appreciated by hosts and may earn you more party invitations in the future.

Make It Happen

➤ The next time you receive an invite, check to see if an RSVP is required. If so, give the hosts a call at your earliest convenience to tell them "yes" or "no", and how many will be attending.

#63: Write a Thank You Note

Everyone likes getting presents. Remembering to send a formal thank you note is a small courtesy that givers will appreciate and might keep you on their list for next time.

Make It Happen

➤ Take time to hand write your thank you on a note card and send it by snail mail. There are lots of inexpensive note cards at discount stores or have fun making your own cards with stamps, stickers, and calligraphy pens.

➤ Delight your reader with a well written thank you note. Be sure to mention the gift by name and the occasion for which it was given.

➢ Be specific about what you liked about the gift or how you plan to use it. Wrap up with a sentence of how you might connect with the giver in the future.

➢ Thank you notes are not limited to gifts. It's good practice to send a note after a job interview, when someone does something helpful for your personal or professional life, and after making an important professional contact.

#64: Make an Introduction

Do you ever feel nervous or awkward about meeting new people? Making an introduction is easy and helps people feel included in a social setting. Knowing how to introduce yourself is important to appear confident and approachable.

Make It Happen

➢ Introduce yourself. In the United States, eye contact is very important as is a pleasant facial expression. Project your voice and say something like "Hello, my name is __" and extend a handshake. The person will likely respond "It's nice to meet you" and smile in return.

➢ Introduce two people to each other. You can say something like "Mrs. Johnson, may I introduce Mrs. Gutierrez?" Give them a little bit of information about each other to help get a conversation started. In business, introduce people by rank, not gender or age. Women and men should stand when introduced, smile, and use eye contact.

#65: Social Networking

Facebook and LinkedIn are popular networking websites that allow people to make friends, display photos, and keep in touch with people on a daily basis. Used properly, these sites can be a lot of fun and a helpful tool for making new contacts.

Make It Happen

- ➤ Before creating a profile, make sure your family is on board with your social networking adventure. Show them how it works by touring a friend's page.

- ➤ Take precautions to protect yourself on the Internet. Set profiles to private to avoid strangers from viewing your information. Never accept a friend request from someone you haven't met in person. Never call or arrange to meet someone you've only talked to online. Never post personal information on your site or wall.

- ➤ Try using the event feature to invite a group of friends to a party. It's quick, keeps track of RSVP's and saves paper.

#66: Table Manners

Burping and slouching at the table are definite no's but are you aware of the other subtle rules of table etiquette? By following a few simple guidelines, you can dine with ease, whether you're attending a formal gathering or just having dinner at a friend's house.

Make It Happen

➤ There are quite a few specific rules around food and table manners so you might find it helpful to refer to an etiquette book or attend a community education class. Grandparents may also be good sources of etiquette advice.

➤ Host a dinner party for friends. Plan a meal with multiple courses so you can challenge your guests on which fork gets used for which purpose. Use real cloth napkins and bring out the finger bowls with lemon for a fancy way to freshen your hands.

➤ Make a reservation at a fine dining restaurant and try out your new skills in public. As soon as you are seated, remove your napkin, unfold it and place it in your lap. Turn off your cell phone during dinner or put it on vibrate. Wait to begin eating until all are served. Leave a tip for your server, customarily between 15-20% of the meal value.

#67: Solve Conflicts with Effective Communication

How you phrase a request can help you gain cooperation from someone or put them on the defense. Using an "I" statement instead of a "You" statement helps the person understand your perspective instead of feeling blamed. Being an active listener lets the person know you are genuinely concerned and hearing their side of the story. This skill works also works well in communicating with parents, friends and siblings.

Make It Happen

➤ Have an issue with your grade in a class? Try advocating for yourself by approaching the teacher directly, instead of asking an adult to handle the situation. Find a quiet time for the conversation and phrase your request respectfully. "I am concerned about ___" is often a good way to start the discussion.

➤ Instead of fighting with your family, set up a meeting to discuss the issue. Choose your timing wisely, not when adults are tired or rushing out the door. Prepare by thinking how your solution might benefit the other party. If your request is not approved, ask what steps you could take to positively influence their decision and then set up a time to review again in the near future.

➤ Having trouble resolving a conflict on your own? Contact a school counselor for help. Counselors have been trained to mediate conflicts and provide helpful resources.

#68: Social Dance

No one wants to feel awkward at social occasions like bar mitzvah's, proms and weddings. Invest in your social self by taking time to learn a few of the classic dance moves. Dancing is also great exercise and an activity you can do with your friends.

Make It Happen

➤ Get inspired by watching some old movies with great dancing like *Grease, Dirty Dancing,* or *Saturday Night Fever.*

➢ Register for a community education ballroom dancing class with some friends. The instructor can show you the basics like how to lead or follow and specific dances like the Salsa, Waltz, and Foxtrot.

➢ Organize a dance party or find a venue that has live music. Bring some friends along and get crazy on the dance floor!

#69: Embrace Diversity

Diversity in thought, culture, religion, gender and many other factors makes for a richer community. Colleges and workplaces want members that value inclusion and have global experiences so take time now to get to know others that are different than you.

Make It Happen

➢ Take a foreign language in school. Most colleges require some foreign language coursework and if you start early enough, you may be able to earn college credits in high school.

➢ Ask if your school offers an international or diversity club. Clubs are a great way to meet new people and develop valuable resume experience for college applications.

➢ Consider hosting an international exchange student. Welcoming a student from another country into your home gives you insight into that culture that you wouldn't get from taking a class. Many host families become lifelong friends with their host students.

#70: Make Good Decisions

Learning to make good decisions takes practice and is a vital skill for young adults. No one wants to get caught off guard and make a bad choice so spend some time upfront thinking about your values and goals in life.

Make It Happen

➤ Make a list of adults (outside your immediate family) that you can talk to for advice. Research shows that the more supportive adults a teen has in their life, the less risky behaviors they will engage in. Teachers, coaches, grandparents, faith communities, neighbors and scout leaders are all potential mentors.

➤ Faced with a tough decision? If you don't have to decide on the spot, define the problem and then brainstorm possible solutions. Ask a trusted adult for feedback before you act. If you feel pressured to decide on the spot, it's OK to tell the person you need time to think. Most people don't make the best decisions when they're in a hurry.

#71: Make a Personal Appointment

Arranging your own doctor or haircut appointment is a step to independence and gives you more control over your schedule. Most personal appointments are made over the phone and you will need your calendar handy to tell the receptionist what time is convenient for your schedule.

Make It Happen

> ➢ The next time you need a haircut, call and make it yourself. Tell the receptionist the reason for your call and be ready to give her the dates and times you would like to come in. If you prefer a certain stylist, let know that as well. Be sure to log your appointment in your personal planner.

> ➢ Not feeling so well? Schedule your own appointment with a doctor. Check with an adult first to make sure you have insurance coverage with that provider. Tell the receptionist the reason for your call and if you prefer to see a certain doctor. Depending on how severe your symptoms are, he will suggest a time for you to come to the office. Note the time and location of the appointment so you can be on time.

#72: Time Management

People with good time management skills get more done with less stress. Although some people enjoy planning more than others, everyone can learn to manage their time effectively. You will feel good about getting a lot accomplished and being on time to events.

Make It Happen

> ➢ Keep track of your daily assignments and activities in a planner or on a family calendar.

> ➢ Have a large project due for school? Don't procrastinate! Jump right in and define a realistic timeframe to complete it. Break the project down into smaller steps and keep track of

your progress in a planner or on the computer. Reward yourself with something special when you meet the deadline.

#73: Just Say "No"

Go with the flow isn't always the best advice when it comes to groups and decision making. Don't feel pressured by your friends to do something you're uncomfortable with. Anticipate situations that could be difficult so you are prepared to say "no" assertively and confidently.

Make It Happen

➢ Spending time with positive peers reduces your chances of encountering tough situations. True friends won't pressure you to do something that could hurt you.

➢ Generate a list of scenarios of where you might encounter peer pressure. Make up a code word or phrase that you can call home with that translates into *I'm in an uncomfortable setting. Please pick me up now.*

➢ Find out if your school has any clubs that promote positive choices like Students Against Destructive Decisions (SADD). Members provide support to each other while working on worthy causes.

#74: Entertain

Whether you're having a sleepover or hosting a birthday party, it's helpful to know the basics of being a good host or hostess. Making your guests feel welcome is the primary goal and will ensure that they want to come back and visit you again.

Make It Happen

> ➤ Invite a friend to stay overnight. Introduce your friend to your family and have something fun planned to do. Offer some snacks and something to drink during the course of the evening.

> ➤ Host a party for a small group of friends. Prepare your food and drinks ahead of time to avoid being stuck in the kitchen when you could be out socializing with your guests. Greet your guests at the door and help make introductions if everyone doesn't already know each other. Spend time with each guest so everyone feels welcome. When it's time to say good bye, be sure to walk each guest to the door.

#75: Manage Anger

Everyone one gets mad sometimes but feeling angry all the time is hard on your body. Learning to manage strong emotions is important to protect your health and maintain good relationships with other people.

Make It Happen

> ➤ Make a list of things that make you mad. Brainstorm ideas on how you could better cope in those situations. For example, if you get really angry when you get stuck in traffic on your way to school, try setting your alarm 15 minutes earlier to beat the morning rush hour.

> ➤ Find ways to reduce your stress and you will be less likely to snap. There are lots of ways to stress less: trade massages with a friend, take a run or work out, or watch a funny movie.

- ➢ Sometimes situations are so intense that it's hard to get your feelings under control. Contact a counselor or therapist for help. Counselors keep your conversations confidential and sometimes just talking with someone can help put things in perspective.

#76: Healthy Relationships

There's nothing better than spending quality time with friends or family. Friends that are caring and trustworthy help support each other through good and bad times. Be a good judge of who is a true friend. Friendship should not be controlling, physically or verbally abusive, or about pressuring someone to do things they are uncomfortable with.

Make It Happen

- ➢ Make good friends by being a good friend. Little gestures show you care so take time to find out your friend's birthday and make a card. If your friend is home from school sick, call him after school and ask how he is feeling.
- ➢ When you are old enough to have a romantic relationship, take care to treat the other person with respect. Expect respect yourself and watch out for signs of an abusive relationship: jealousy or possessiveness, attempts to control you or isolate you from family or friends, displays of temper or violence. If you feel you are in an unsafe or questionable relationship, seek help from a trusted adult immediately.

Get Connected Resources

Boys and Girls Clubs of America www.bgca.org

Boys and Girls Club is a neighborhood based club focused solely on youth programs and activities that teach kids the skills they need to succeed in life.

Emily Post Institute www.emilypost.com

From social networking to social graces, Emily Post has been the definitive source on etiquette for generations of Americans.

MyHealth www.myhealthmn.org

MyHealth offers professional, low cost medical, mental health and health education to teens 12-23 in Hennepin, Carver and Scott counties of Minnesota.

Red Cross www.redcross.org

The Red Cross helps with disaster relief and offers training and community programs.

Teens Alone www.teensalone.org

Teens Alone provide confidential and free counseling and crisis services to families in the western suburbs of Minneapolis.

The Bridge for Youth www.bridgeforyouth.org

The Bridge for Youth offers a full range of services from hotline and emergency services to longer term housing, family reunification and life skills.

Going for the Gold

11

Sports and Fitness

"The most rewarding things you do in life are often the ones
that look like they cannot be done."
~ Arnold Palmer

Whether you're a Zumba enthusiast or a hockey fan, sports and fitness is a big part of American culture. Find a team to cheer for or take up a sport yourself. Bonding together with teammates over a common goal is a natural way to make new friends and is rewarding no matter if you win or lose. Individual pursuits like yoga or tennis are also wonderful ways to get active and look your best. Chapter 11 identifies eight critical competencies students should know in the sports and fitness arena.

#77: Play on a Team

There is more to sports than knowing how to play the game. Work ethic, perseverance, good sportsmanship, getting along with others, and respect are all learned on the playing field and are valuable foundations for life.

Make It Happen

➢ If you have not already experienced a team sport, give one a try. Check your school website to see what sports are offered. By high school, many sports are competitive but community leagues are a nice alternative for brand new players.

➢ Already a seasoned player? Take on a leadership role. Join the student board or offer to chair a fundraising event. Colleges like to see leadership experience within your favorite activities.

#78: Good Sportsmanship

Have you ever witnessed a golfer throwing a club across the green or a softball player yelling back at the ref? These examples of bad sportsmanship reflect poorly on the player and detract from the joy of the game. Showing appropriate respect for officials and other players, sharing the limelight with teammates, and congratulating the losing team after the game are ways to demonstrate your maturity. Coaches prefer to work with players that can handle themselves professionally on and off the field.

Make It Happen

➢ Analyze your game behavior. Are there certain situations that continue to cause you frustration? Try to take positive action instead of letting the situation control you. For example, if putting is ruining your game, arrange for a private lesson and work on your technique.

➢ Be a good role model. Compliment a new teammate on their game performance or be the first in line to congratulate the other team. Your positive actions can inspire others to do the same.

#79: Know Thy BMI

Body Mass Index (BMI) is a calculation that compares your height to your weight. It's a helpful tool to gauge whether your weight is within the normal range for your height. Maintaining a healthy weight is one of the best things you can do to take charge of your health and live a longer life.

Make It Happen

➢ Perform the calculation. The formula for BMI is weight, divided by height squared, multiplied by 703. A BMI between 18-25 is considered in the normal range.

➢ If you scored above 25, talk with your doctor. She may suggest a healthy eating plan or ways to incorporate exercise into your daily routine.

#80: Calculate Your Heart Rate

Enjoy a good workout? Knowing your target heart rate zone is important to maximize your workout and achieve your fitness goals.

Make It Happen

➢ Calculate your target heart rate zone. First find your maximum heart rate which is 220 minus your age. Then find your target heart rate which is 65-85% of your maximum heart rate.

➢ Check your heart rate while exercising. Take your pulse and compare the beats per minute to your target heart rate. A general rule of thumb is that your workout should be light enough so that you can talk but vigorous enough so that you could not sing a song.

#81: Swim

Jumping in the lake on a hot summer day can be one of summer's greatest pleasures, assuming you know how to swim. There are many fun activities to do if you are comfortable in the water like boating, water skiing, and snorkeling. Beyond the benefits of exercise, learning to swim is an important safety skill.

Make It Happen

➢ If your swimming skills are not the best, take some lessons. Most school districts offer lessons or you can contact the American Red Cross.

➢ If you are already a competent swimmer, consider becoming a life guard or water safety aide. Take a certification class to learn advanced skills and life saving techniques including CPR. You may be able to score a summer job as a life guard at a local pool or beach.

#82: Ride a Bike

Riding a bike takes balance, coordination and endurance. In many parts of the world biking is the best way to navigate the city. Bicycles don't require gas, keep you in shape and are good for the planet.

Make It Happen

> ➤ Find a decent used bike and try biking to school or work on nice days. Check out ads online or call your local bike shop to see if they have a trade in sale.

> ➤ Register for a cycling race with a group of friends to benefit a good cause. The United Way often has public races that help raise money for nonprofit organizations.

#83: Exercise

Do you like to do aerobics and workout at the gym or do you find yourself curling up on the couch after school or spending hours at the computer playing video games? Experts recommend 60 minutes or more of moderate to vigorous physical activity daily. Exercise is one of the best things you can do to optimize your weight, feel good, and live longer.

Make It Happen

> ➤ Take a walk. Borrow a pedometer and track how many steps you take in a day. Health professionals recommend 10,000

steps each day. Bring a friend, walk a pet, take your music and hit the streets.

➤ Try something new like yoga or badminton. It's easy to get in an exercise rut and lose your enthusiasm for working out. Keeping it fresh challenges your brain and your body.

#84: Sports Savvy

So much of our culture revolves around sports that it pays to have a basic knowledge of the rules and objectives of major sports. Casual conversations often begin with some kind of small talk about the weather or sports. You don't have to play a sport to be sports savvy. Doing a little research on the game and the players can help keep you in the loop later on.

Make It Happen

➤ Make a list of sports you are least familiar with. Look on the Internet or ask a friend who plays the game for an explanation of the objectives, rules, and top players.

➤ Go to a game. Tickets to high school sports are a bargain and admission to games in most community leagues is free.

➤ Check out a sports magazine or read the sports section in your local paper. Scan the articles and be ready to discuss the game score or newest recruit with your friends or family.

Get Connected Resources

Centers for Disease Control and Prevention

www.cdc.gov/healthyweight/assessing/index.html

An agency of the U.S. Department of Public Safety, the CDC provides information on public health issues affecting the United States. The site has a helpful section on achieving a healthy weight, complete with an online BMI calculator.

Let's Move www.letsmove.gov

Let's Move! is a comprehensive initiative, launched by Michelle Obama, dedicated to solving the problem of obesity within a generation. The site has lots of tips for healthy eating and increasing physical activity.

National Collegiate Athletic Association www.ncaa.org

The National Collegiate Athletic Association is a membership-driven organization dedicated to safeguarding the well-being of student athletes. Visit the site for information on D1, D2, D3 recruiting, a calendar of signing dates, scholarships and eligibility rules.

TeensHealth www.kidshealth.org/teen

TeensHealth is part of the KidsHealth family of websites run by the nonprofit Nemours Center for Children's Health Media. It provides accurate information that is free of medical jargon.

YMCA www.ymca.org

YMCA's mission is to build strong kids, strong families, and communities. They offer youth development programs including Black Achievers, sports, camps and Youth and Government.

Surfing in San Diego

Finals?

12

Technology

"Never trust anything that can think for itself
if you can't see where it keeps its brain."
~ *J.K. Rowling*

Today's teens have grown up with technology and are often the IT experts at home. Most parents worry about their child's safety in cyberspace so demonstrating you can do so responsibly will help ensure you maintain access to the cell phones and computers you've come to depend on. Chapter 12 presents seven technology skills that students should master including Internet safety, electronic communications, and basic computer software.

#85: Cell Phone Savvy

Cell phones are great tools for keeping in touch. New models are full of functionality from making a simple call to taking pictures, texting, and checking emails. They are helpful to have in an emergency and are a good way to help parents relax because they can reach you at all times.

Make It Happen

➢ Use proper cell phone etiquette. Make sure your phone is off or on vibrate in certain settings like school, work, the dinner table, place of worship, etc. Don't use your cell and drive. Take your calls privately or use a quiet tone of voice when answering a call in public.

➢ Friends love to take pictures of each other on their cell phones but be aware of who might be snapping a picture of you. Unflattering pictures can be downloaded to the Internet instantly and forwarded to large groups of people. Be a good example by not participating in Internet bullying.

➢ Due to their popularity and small size, cell phones can be stolen and resold before you notice your device is even missing. Safeguard your phone by registering it on security network. In public, be especially aware as phones left on a library desk or even those carefully stowed in backpacks have been known to disappear.

#86: Utilize Email

Email is commonly used by workplaces, teams and community groups to facilitate communication. It is an easy, quick way to send a message and attachment to a group of people. Save on paper and postage by using this electronic form of communication.

Make It Happen

➢ Consider setting up separate email accounts for different purposes. Your *partylikearockstar123* address is better used for emailing friends and not potential employers or college admission officers. Play it safe by choosing a more conservative address for professional communications.

➢ Invest in reliable virus software. Protect your computer from viruses by not opening email attachments from unknown sources. Use email filters to avoid being bothered by junk mail.

#87: Use a Word Processing Program

Learning to type and use a word processing program like Microsoft Word is a critical skill for today's students. Creating a document on the computer allows you to make easy revisions and use special effects. A typed project also looks neater and is easier to read which might result in a better grade.

Make It Happen

➢ If you're still typing *hunt and peck* style, take a keyboarding class. You will learn techniques on hand position and how to increase your typing speed and accuracy.

> ➤ Experiment with Word's advanced features like formatting or auto shapes. Get creative with your document using colors and clipart.

#88: Use a Spreadsheet Program

The beauty of a spreadsheet program like Excel is that it does math for you at the speed of lightening. You can use a spreadsheet for projects where you need to add, subtract, multiple or divide. Employers value computer literacy so possessing this skill may give you an advantage when applying for a job.

Make It Happen

> ➤ If you haven't used Excel before, experiment with the basic features to create a simple spreadsheet. For example, you can track your expenses by category to see where your money is being spent.

> ➤ Take an Excel class through your local community education department to learn more advanced techniques like graphs and charts. Update your resume to showcase your new skill.

#89: Use a Presentation Program

A presentation program like PowerPoint is ideal for creating attractive slides for school projects or other presentations. Use a template or create your own look using inserted clip art, numerous fonts and colors. Last minute changes are easy to make by inserting a slide or updating text. Most formal presentations given today use computer visuals so getting comfortable with this technology will enhance your professional image.

Make It Happen

➤ Practice creating a short presentation. Compare the look of a template to one that you create from scratch. Keep font size readable and don't crowd too many words onto one slide.

➤ Take a PowerPoint class to learn how to incorporate some advanced features into your presentations. Have fun trying out options like animation or sound.

#90: Use a Search Engine

Google has become a household word and is one of the main search engines on the Internet. Type in a key word or phrase and the search engine will return a list of websites that relate to your topic. This resource is a must for school research projects but is also helpful for everyday life to find phone numbers, check out a college, shop online, see what movie is playing and much more.

Make It Happen

➤ Experiment on Google by typing in different key words for the same topic. What results come up? Depending on your search you may choose to use a more general term or be more specific.

#91: Cyber Safety

The Internet is one of the greatest inventions in the last century. From the convenience of your own computer you can do research, send emails, and connect with friends. It's easy to forget that the Internet is a public place so keep up your guard. Protect yourself by using the same safety precautions you would if you were encountering a stranger in person.

Make It Happen

- ➢ If you have a social networking page, protect your online identity by making your profile private. Don't share your password with anyone other than a trusted adult, including your girlfriend or boyfriend. If someone logs on as you, they could read your messages or trash your profile. Remember that even with a private setting, your pictures and content could be copied and forwarded to the masses, so review your page and make sure even grandma would approve.

- ➢ Review your social networking page as if you were a future employer and remove any unprofessional content.

- ➢ Guard your personal information. Don't post your phone number, address, social security number or other data that could make it easy for a stranger to target you or your family. Keep online friendships virtual and do not agree to meet an online friend in person without having a trusted adult accompany you. The 16 year old girl you think you've been talking to could easily be a 50 year old man with a prison record.

Get Connected Resources

GetNetWise www.getnetwise.org

GetNetWise is a project of the Internet Education Foundation that promotes safe and educational online experiences. The site has an Internet safety guide with tips by age, risks by type and technology and tools for families.

Protect My Rep www.protectmyrep.org

Creation of 360 Journalism, a youth journalism program at the University of St. Thomas, St. Paul, MN. Includes tips on social media, who's watching, how to protect yourself and how to repair your reputation.

StopBullying.gov www.stopbullying.gov

This site provides information from various government agencies on what bullying is, what cyber bullying is, who is at risk, and how you can prevent and respond to bullying.

Teenangels www.teenangels.org

Teenangels are 13 to 18 year old volunteers that have been specially trained by the founder of WiredSafety in online safety, privacy and security.

Exchange student from Brazil

13

The World of Work

"Choose a job you love, and you will never have to work
a day in your life."
~ Confucius

Do you know what you want to be when you grow up? That's a tough question even for some adults but there are steps you can take now to help you be ready when the time comes. A part-time job is a practical way to test your abilities and see if you enjoy a particular work environment. Networking and mentoring are great support systems too. Chapter 13 identifies nine career-related competencies that prepare students to be *workforce ready* including tips on writing a resume, using effective business communication, and creating a professional image.

#92: Create a Resume

A resume is a summary of your accomplishments and activities. A well thought out resume highlights your special qualities and gives colleges and employers a snapshot about what kind of person you are and if you would be a good fit for their organization. Having a resume ready to go allows you to be ready for opportunities and it's also fun to read over the things you do so well!

Make It Happen

➢ Start keeping track of your activities in middle school. Note the activity name, supervising adult, dates of participation and hours completed.

➢ Create a formal resume highlighting your accomplishments at school, your work history, community service and special strengths. There are many resume builders on the Internet. Ask several people to help you proofread your document so you are positive there are no grammar or punctuation errors.

➢ Review your resume on your birthday or at the end of each school year and update your accomplishments.

#93: Interview for a Job

Ready to apply for a part-time job? Brush up on your interview skills so you are well prepared and confident. Employers generally look for candidates who are eager to work, have relevant skills, and are a good fit for the company's culture. Landing your first job is a milestone and it's empowering to start earning your own money.

Make It Happen

➢ Make a list of your strengths and weaknesses. These are typical questions in an interview so it's good to be prepared. Think about how you could phrase a weakness as a strength instead.

➢ Update your resume with your latest accomplishments and customize the layout to the particular job you are applying for. For example, if you have an interview at a child care center, be sure to include any experience you have in caring for children.

➢ Practice with a friend. Interviewers tend to ask common questions like *Why do you want to work here?* and *What are your strengths and weaknesses?* For the actual interview, bring a resume, be on time, and dress for success.

#94: Work a Part-Time Job

Getting your first part-time job is exciting and a great way to learn new skills. Take time to find a good match for your interests and schedule. While many colleges like to see work experience, they also value grades and community service, so be careful not to take on too many hours at the expense of other activities.

Make It Happen

➢ Do an interest analysis. What are your strengths? What do you enjoy doing in your free time? The ideal job will make use of your natural abilities in an environment you enjoy. If you are undecided, many high school guidance counselors offer free career surveys to help point you in the right direction.

➢ Conduct a job search. Check your high school website for job postings. You can also network with friends, family, neighbors, and community members to find job openings.

➢ Be proactive in contacting potential employers. If you find a place you'd really like to work, give the manager a call and ask to schedule an informational interview to find out more about that workplace and its opportunities. A face to face meeting just might result in a job offer at a later date.

#95: Give a Presentation

According to many studies, people's number one fear is public speaking. Whether you are a student or an employee in the workplace, most people will eventually need to speak in front of a group. Being able to get your point across clearly and connect with your audience are skills that will help you appear confident and credible.

Make It Happen

➢ Do your research. Before you can explain something to others, you must understand it well yourself.

➢ Use technology to illustrate your points. PowerPoint and video clips are just a couple of tools presenters can use to liven up their presentations. Ask your technology education teacher for the newest tips and tricks.

➢ Practice with friends and family and ask for their feedback. Does your presentation have a logical flow? Does it appeal to your audience? Are you using good eye contact and not speaking too fast? Don't memorize your speech but be comfortable with the main points and timing.

#96: **Write a Professional Email**

Texting and social networking are good ways to contact friends but knowing how to write a professional email is a necessary skill to connect with adults. Email is less formal than a written letter and reaches the recipient much faster.

Make It Happen

➢ Write a practice email and ask a business education teacher for feedback. Greetings are typically simple: *Hello* vs. the formal *Dear Mr. Smith* that you would find in a business letter. Write out words instead of using texting abbreviations. Include a telephone number with the email signature so the recipient can contact you by phone if desired. Use the spell check feature and proof read for other errors that spell check doesn't catch.

➢ Before college application time, consider upgrading your email name to one that sounds more professional.

#97: **Dress for Business**

Dressing appropriately for the occasion is important if you want to look your best and impress a potential employer or college admissions officer. Professional style is the most conservative and would be appropriate for a formal college interview or a job interview with a conservative company. Business casual style is more relaxed and is now common in many workplaces.

Make It Happen

➤ Consider investing in one professional outfit and one business casual outfit so you are prepared when a job interview or college tour opportunity arises.

➤ Check your interview outfit and ask a working adult for feedback. Are you wearing flip flops? Jeans? Lip ring? Chains? Better to stay with a conservative choice and save your trendy gear for nights out with your friends.

#98: Business Handshake

Greet someone new with a firm handshake and you're on your way to making a good first impression. Before extending your hand, introduce yourself. Make eye contact and smile and you will come across as confident and approachable.

Make It Happen

➤ Practice your handshake on your family to get your timing down. Strive for a firm grip (not too forceful or limp) and shake the hand two to three times.

➤ Try out your business handshake on an adult and watch their reaction. Use this technique when meeting a friend's parents or teachers for the first time and they will be impressed with your friendliness and maturity.

#99: Network

It's not what you know, it's who you know. Most teens are familiar with Facebook and Twitter but knowing how to network goes beyond using these popular sites. While it may sound intimidating, networking is really just meeting new people through someone you both know.

Make It Happen

➢ Hoping to score a summer job with a specific company? Schedule an informational interview a few months before school gets out. An information interview is a chance to introduce yourself and ask questions about the company and the jobs they offer. If you discover this is the ideal place you'd like to work, you've already made a connection when it comes time to apply.

➢ Joining a group is an easy way to network and meet people outside your social circle. Look for opportunities with school clubs like DECA, faith community youth groups or community organizations like Boys and Girls Clubs.

➢ Adults use the website LinkedIn as a tool for business related networking. Become familiar with this site by asking an adult to show you their profile and connections so you are ready to create your own profile when you turn 18.

#100: Go Global

If you've traveled internationally or had the opportunity to meet someone from another country, you've probably noticed differences between cultures. Although we may live in different places or speak different languages, *people are people* and it's fun to discover that we have things in common too. Understanding and appreciating diversity is a great way to enjoy new places and make new friends.

Make It Happen

➤ Invite a student from another country to live with your family for a semester or school year. There are many quality programs that can coordinate the match and offer support throughout the stay. If you are learning a language in school, choose someone from that country and you will have a partner to practice speaking with. If hosting a student is not an option, get to know one of the exchange students who is already at your school. If you are very adventurous, apply to be an international exchange student yourself!

➤ Food is an important part of every culture. Research ethnic restaurants, and go out to eat with your friends. Try a spicy Thai dish, authentic Mexican churros, or Greek pitas and you may find a new favorite food!

➤ Students in other countries often speak multiple languages. If you are lucky enough to speak two languages in your household, keep up the good work! If you haven't mastered a second language, it's not too late to start. Register for the next semester or learn on your own through a software program like Rosetta Stone.

Get Connected Resources

BestPrep www.bestprep.org

BestPrep's mission is to best prepare Minnesota students with business, career and financial literacy skills through experiences that inspire success in work and life.

ClearCause Foundation www.clearcausefoundation.org

ClearCause provides tools and information to help parents, youth and chaperones identify risks and take positive steps to mitigate these risks abroad. This site has recommendations on program safety guidelines, comprehensive stay safe information and emergency preparedness plans.

DECA www.deca.org

DECA prepares emerging leaders and entrepreneurs in marketing, finance, hospitality and management in high schools and colleges across the globe.

Junior Achievement www.ja.org

JA is the world's largest organization dedicated to educating students about workforce readiness, entrepreneurship and financial literacy through experiential, hands-on programs.

LinkedIn www.linkedin.com

The mission of LinkedIn is to connect the world's professionals to enable them to be more productive and successful: meet, exchange ideas, learn, make deals, find opportunities or employees, work, and make decisions in a network of trusted relationships and groups.

Rotary International www.rotary.org

Rotary's programs for students and youth can change the lives of those who participate. Through these programs, young people can earn scholarships, travel on cultural exchanges, or help a community through a service project.

Goldy Gopher

14

Campus Collections

"The journey of a thousand miles begins with one step."
~ Lao Tzu

It's exciting and a little nerve-racking to go on your first college visit. We've put together some tools to make this process easier so you can relax and focus on what's most important—finding a college that's the right fit for you!

College Scorecard

College Visit Checklist

25 Ways to Start Saving for College

Spotlight on Scholarships

25 Ways to Make a Difference

25 Ways to Develop Leadership Skills

College Scorecard

Take time to record your impressions so you'll remember the highlights of each school you visit. You are welcome to print this scorecard: www.partnersinparentingconsulting.com.

College Scorecard: Campus Overview

Date of Visit

College Name

City, State

Distance from Home

Students

Private or Public

Rural or Suburban or City

Student to Staff Ratio

Average Class Size

Average ACT score

Average SAT score

Sticker Price including tuition/room/board/fees

Size of Endowment Fund

Net Price including average financial aid award

Things I like most about this school are:

Things that bother me about this school are:

Some questions I still have about this school are:

College Scorecard: Campus Features

Rate each feature from low (1) to high (5)

Cafeteria

_____ Variety of appealing food choices
_____ Convenience
_____ Dietary accommodations
_____ Food quality and taste
_____ Organic or locally grown offerings

Location

_____ Proximity to home
_____ Fun things to do on and off campus
_____ Weather
_____ Aesthetics

Academics

_____ Majors that interest me
_____ School year calendar
_____ Professors and teaching assistants
_____ Special programs

Sports

_____ Offers my sport(s)
_____ Coaching staff
_____ Athletic facilities
_____ Reputation

Housing

_____ Dorm room size
_____ Dorm bathrooms
_____ Dorm common areas
_____ Dorm locks, smoke/CO2 detectors, visitor policies
_____ Upper classman housing options

Culture

_____ Diversity of students/staff
_____ Special traditions
_____ Fraternities/sororities
_____ Clubs and service opportunities

Sustainability

_____ Recycling in dorms and common buildings
_____ Low flow shower heads and toilets
_____ Energy efficient initiatives
_____ Food composting, tray-less dining, Styrofoam free
_____ Chemical free lawns, rain gardens, native plants

Admissions

_____ Welcoming atmosphere
_____ Ability to answer questions
_____ Entrance requirements match with my profile

Cost

_____ Percent of students that receive financial/merit aid
_____ Percent of students that graduate in four years
_____ Extra amenities included in tuition
_____ Cost to go home
_____ Scholarships
_____ Net Price

Total Score: __ / 200

College Visit Checklist

Make the most of your visit to campus with these helpful tips:

- ✓ Take a campus tour and ask to see the dorms

- ✓ Interview with an admissions counselor

- ✓ Eat lunch in the cafeteria

- ✓ Attend a college sporting event

- ✓ Inquire about scholarships at the financial aid office

- ✓ Meet with a coach of the sport you plan to play in college

- ✓ Strike up a conversation with current students

- ✓ Read the posters in the dorms and building hallways

- ✓ Arrange to sit in on a class

- ✓ Explore the athletic facility

- ✓ Take a drive around the city surrounding campus

- ✓ Browse through the campus bookstore

- ✓ Check out the nightlife on campus

- ✓ Stay overnight in a dorm

- ✓ Fill out *Campus Collections* College Scorecard

- ✓ Write thank you notes

25 Ways to Start Saving for College

It's never too early to start saving for college! Average annual total charges for a private nonprofit four year college in 2013-14 were $40,917. We're not sharing that figure to scare you but want to motivate you to action. Aside from earning money, colleges love to see students that take the initiative to help finance their education. We've brainstormed some fun ways to help you get started.

1. Open your own savings account

2. Start a 529 college savings plan

3. Decorate a jar and throw in your spare change

4. Babysit for neighborhood families

5. Apply early for summer job opportunities

6. Dig out your old junk and host a garage sale

7. Hold a car wash at a local gas station

8. Arrange a Parents' Night Out event with childcare

9. Organize a day camp for neighborhood kids

10. Deposit part of each paycheck directly into your savings

11. Start your own lawn raking or snow shoveling service

12. Attend a financial aid seminar with your family

13. Offer tutoring services

14. Host a holiday bake sale

15. Start your own pet walking service or doggy day care

16. Negotiate an allowance raise for an extra set of chores

17. Trade in old clothes or home goods for cash

18. Invite friends and family to a *Cook for College* BBQ

19. Coordinate an arts and crafts sale

20. Skip one treat each week and save the money instead

21. Advertise your services as a kids' birthday party assistant

22. Put birthday or holiday money directly into your savings

23. Organize a dog wash

24. Host a *Concert for College* event with your musical friends

25. Start your own housecleaning business

Spotlight on Scholarships

A recent study by Fidelity Investments found that 70% of the class of 2013 graduated with $35,200 in college-related debt. Fortunately, there are steps you can take now to combat the rising costs of a college education.

Scholarships are a creative way to supplement your college financing. They differ from loans in that they are *free money* and do not need to be paid back. There are thousands of opportunities—merit competitions that reward good grades or community service, grants on financial need, essay contests, school scholarships, and local and national competitions. We've gathered our best tips to share with you – best of luck in your scholarship search!

1. Many colleges offer scholarships for involvement in music, dance, speech, leadership and good grades. Your odds of scoring a grant through a college who wants to recruit you are much greater than winning a national competition so start your search here.

2. Ask your family if their workplace offers scholarships for employees' children. If you are part of a faith community, inquire about opportunities there as well.

3. Full ride sports scholarships are the GREAT EXCEPTION to the rule. The NCAA reports that only 2% of qualified students receive a partial sports scholarship so keep up your GPA even if you a star athlete.

4. Make an appointment with your school counselor to review the scholarships offered through your high school. Bring a list of things that set you apart from other applicants like ethnicity, child of a veteran, deceased parent, Eagle or Gold award recipient, etc.

5. Use a free search site like School Soup or Chegg to identify national contests that best match your background.

6. NEVER pay a fee to apply for a scholarship. Reputable programs do not charge money.

7. It's easy to become overwhelmed with opportunities so take time to get organized first. Create a folder for each application, write the due date on the cover, and highlight any special requirements. Keep a copy of the application for your records.

8. Here's the weirdest scholarship we've found so far:

DUCK® BRAND TAPE *STUCK AT PROM®*

Participants must attend a school prom wearing complete prom attire made using Duck® Brand Duct Tape. They must describe in 1,000 characters or less how they created their prom night outfits and how many hours they spent. Winner is awarded a $5000 scholarship and $5000 for the school. More details at www.duckbrand.com.

25 Ways to Make a Difference

"Life's most persistent and urgent question is
'What are you doing for others?'"
~ Dr. Martin Luther King, Jr.

Volunteering your time is a great way to meet new people and gain valuable experience you can draw on at college application time. Anyone can lend a hand and we've put together a list of ideas to spark your interest. You can do it—get started today!

1. Volunteer at a local food shelf on days off from school

2. Chaperone a younger group of kids on Halloween

3. Prepare a meal at a local crisis shelter

4. Adopt a local park

5. Collect pop cans and bring them to a recycling center

6. Help out at a 4th of July community celebration

7. Make welcome baskets for new students

8. Organize a collection of holiday gifts for teens

9. Provide support at a Special Olympics event

10. Celebrate Arbor Day by planting a tree or flowers

11. Visit a veteran's home and thank those who served

12. Mentor a younger child

13. Make valentines for residents at a local senior center

14. Participate in a run or walk for your favorite cause

15. Serve dinner at a local soup kitchen

16. Adopt a grandfriend at a local nursing home

17. Write letters to military personnel serving overseas

18. Celebrate Earth Day by picking up trash with your friends

19. Plant a garden and donate the produce to a local food shelf

20. Assist at a local animal shelter

21. Tutor someone learning English as a second language

22. Teach computer skills at a nearby senior center

23. Mow, rake, or shovel for a homebound neighbor

24. Join a group doing a home improvement project

25. Be a small group leader at a day camp

25 Ways to Develop Leadership Skills

Today's youth are tomorrow's leaders. In just five years, today's seventh graders will be seniors in high school, and today's juniors will be graduating from college. You might think leadership only pertains to the class president or the CEO of a Fortune 500 company, but everyone can develop this important skill in their own way. Colleges and workplaces seek out applicants with leadership experience so don't delay. Whether you like music or technology or sports or the outdoors, we've come up with a list of suggestions—pick one to try out today!

1. Serve on a youth advisory committee

2. Pay it forward by surprising someone with an unexpected kindness

3. Join a community organization like Scouting or 4H

4. Apply for membership in National Honor Society

5. Attend a leadership themed conference or summer camp

6. Host a foreign exchange student

7. Be a foreign exchange student

8. Mentor a child

9. Serve on a junior board of directors

10. Tutor a fellow student

11. Cast your vote during student elections

12. Run for student council

13. Organize a neighborhood improvement project

14. Find a cause you are passionate about and volunteer

15. Audition for a lead role in a play or concert

16. Stick up for someone who is being bullied

17. Take a risk and try something new

18. Participate in a mission trip

19. Coach a kids' sports team

20. Teach a class at senior center

21. Start a new club at school

22. Lead a small group of students in your faith community

23. Welcome new neighbors with fresh baked goodies

24. JUST SAY NO in the face of peer pressure

25. Seek out a mentor

Congratulations Graduate!!

15

My Milestone Map

"Step with care and great tact,
and remember that life's a great balancing act."
~ Dr. Seuss

Congratulations! You reached the end of this book and are now filled with college knowledge. Perhaps you read a section or two that caught your interest, then fast forwarded to the last chapter for the cliff notes conclusion. Feel like you still need some help finding your way through the college admission maze? Keep reading—we promise, we've saved the best for last!

My Milestone Map identifies the important steps in the admission timeline as well as actions your can take to master the Top 100 College Competencies®. The tool was designed for busy students (and parents) and is intended to help you stay on track for graduation.

It's simple and easy to use—one comprehensive calendar to chart your progress:

- Map begins in sixth grade with valuable suggestions on developing good study habits, reading and saving for college.

- Middle school milestones focus on developing College Competencies® and engaging in community service opportunities.

- Milestones become more detailed in high school with suggestions on leadership development and tasks focused on college applications.

- Exact timing of milestones may differ for each student. For example, a student with extremely high standard test scores may begin taking college entrance exams in middle school, where another student would take these tests in high school. A private college coach or your school counselor is a great resource for individualized guidance.

My Milestone Map
Sixth Grade

Whether you're in middle school or junior high, it's not too early to start putting a plan in place for college. You're also at a great age to become more independent by mastering the first of the College Competencies®.

☐ Take the Quiz (www.partnersinparentingconsulting.com) and see which of the 10 subject areas you need to work on.

☐ Choose at least one College Competency from each subject area to develop this year.

☐ Strong study skills are key to getting good grades. Start off on the right foot by buying a planner and using it to keep organized. It's also important to find a distraction free place to do homework.

☐ Read, Read, Read. Whether you like sports or wizards or historical fiction, there are books and magazines for every interest. Check out the new titles at your library.

☐ Start saving for college. It's easy to get started by opening your own savings account.

My Milestone Map

Seventh Grade

Now is the time to start getting involved in your community. Look beyond your school walls to find interesting opportunities where you can volunteer your time.

- ☐ It's empowering to be independent so choose five College Competencies® to work on over the next year.

- ☐ Take the most challenging classes you can handle. Colleges notice when students complete rigorous coursework so ask your guidance counselor to recommend some options.

- ☐ Join an organization where you can develop community service experience. Volunteering your time for a cause you care about is fun!

- ☐ Students with high standard test scores should ask their guidance counselor about taking a college entrance exam (ACT or SAT) in middle school.

- ☐ Read and relax. Reading is a healthy alternative to screen time.

☐ Save for college by picking up ad-hoc jobs like babysitting for neighborhood families.

My Milestone Map
Eighth Grade

Eighth grade is the perfect time to explore your interests and gain valuable service and leadership experience. Keep acquiring College Competencies® and you'll be well prepared for high school.

☐ Review your list of College Competencies®. How many have you mastered so far? Set a goal to complete at least one competency from each subject area this year.

☐ Discover your passion. Brainstorm a list of things you care deeply about, ideas that energize you, social causes you feel strongly about, and local/global issues you want to see solved.

☐ Seek out leadership and community service opportunities that support your passion. Check your school's website for a list or organizations that might need help.

☐ Read up on one of your newly discovered passions. You won't ever be bored if you have a good book.

☐ Save for college by starting a 529 plan.

My Milestone Map
Freshman Year

Congratulations! You're officially in high school—time to get serious since grades now officially count toward your GPA.

September

☐ Get off to a good start. Find a comfortable, quiet place to study and hit the books!

☐ Check out your school's sports and club offerings. Joining a group is a great way to meet new people.

☐ One of the selection criteria for National Honor Society is service. Start earning volunteer hours early in your high school career.

October

- ☐ Stop by your school's office if you haven't met your guidance counselor yet. Counselors' schedules are usually busy so make your appointment today!

- ☐ Camping is a good way to develop the *Eco Adventure Competencies*. Practice *Leaving No Trace* or *Navigating* while you enjoy the fall colors.

- ☐ Keep saving for college idea: start your own lawn raking business.

November

- ☐ Keep studying. Get help early on if there is a class you are struggling with. Most teachers are available before or after class for extra help.

- ☐ Celebrate Thanksgiving Day with friends and family. Develop the *Household (Help!) Competencies* by making a new recipe to share at a holiday gathering.

- ☐ Volunteer idea: collect Thanksgiving themed food for your local food shelf.

December

☐ Enjoy winter vacation and catch up much needed sleep. Sleep is one of the *Health and Happiness Competencies.*

☐ Update your resume noting any new activities, special awards, leadership activities and volunteer hours.

☐ Keep saving for college idea: put a portion of holiday gift money into your college account.

January

☐ How many College Competencies® have you acquired? Make a New Year's resolution to learn ten more this year.

☐ Meet with your guidance counselor to begin planning courses for sophomore year. Take required courses early on to give yourself more flexibility senior year.

☐ Volunteer idea: adopt a grandfriend at a local nursing home.

February

☐ Ask your guidance counselor if you should register for the SAT Subject tests this spring.

☐ If you are a talented athlete, consider attending a skills development camp this summer. Registrations for popular enrichment activities take place early so don't delay!

☐ Keep saving for college idea: negotiate an allowance raise for an extra set of chores.

March

☐ Now that the weather is warming up, get outside and get active! Try calculating your BMI and heart rate to establish a fitness baseline.

☐ Review the list of *Show Me the Money Competencies* and pick two to master.

☐ Volunteer idea: participate in a walk for your favorite cause.

April

☐ Turning 15 soon? Register to take driver's education this summer. Learning to drive a car is one of the *Get Around Town Competencies.*

☐ Baseball games start in April so brush up on the words to the National Anthem.

☐ Keep saving for college idea: clean out your old junk and host a garage sale.

May

☐ Take SAT Subject tests if recommended by your guidance counselor.

- ☐ Volunteer idea: participate in a home building project like Habitat for Humanity.

- ☐ Explore the *Cell Phone Savvy Competency*.

June

- ☐ Celebrate your achievements! Take time to document your accomplishments and volunteer hours on your resume.

- ☐ Visit your local library and check out the summer's hottest new books.

- ☐ Keep saving for college idea: host a car wash at a gas station.

July

- ☐ Summer is a great time to get outdoors and explore. Take a day trip with your family or friends while you are developing one of the *Eco Adventure Competencies*.

- ☐ Volunteer idea: plant a garden and donate the produce to your local food shelf.

- ☐ Browse your local bookstore for great teen reads and keep reading.

August

☐ Check to see if any of your fall classes have summer reading assignments and if so, get a jump start on the books. If not, enjoy choosing your own title.

☐ Set your alarm clock back one week before school starts so your body clock can adjust to waking up early again.

☐ Keep saving for college idea: coordinate an arts and crafts sale.

My Milestone Map
Sophomore Year

With a year of high school behind you, approach your sophomore year with confidence. This is a perfect time to explore your interests and build up a solid GPA.

September

☐ Meet with your guidance counselor. Let him know if your classes are going well or if you are feeling overwhelmed. Counselors can also recommend clubs or activities that appeal to your interests.

- ☐ Make a list of colleges that look interesting and do some preliminary research. Choose one to visit over fall break and schedule an admissions appointment.
- ☐ Keep saving for college idea: attend a financial aid seminar with your family.

October

- ☐ Take on a leadership role in your sport or club. This experience shows colleges you have initiative.
- ☐ Visit a college and record your impressions in the College Scorecard.
- ☐ Volunteer idea: chaperone a group of younger kids on Halloween night.

November

- ☐ Spend extra time studying this month.
- ☐ If art is your thing, start saving your best pieces for a portfolio you can bring to college interviews.
- ☐ Keep saving for college idea: host a holiday bake sale.

December

- ☐ Curl up with a good book over winter break and enjoy some downtime from the usual busy schedule.

- ☐ Take advantage of days off from school to get active outside—try kite skiing, skating, sledding, skijoring, snowshoeing.

- ☐ Volunteer idea: shovel the driveway or sidewalk of an elderly neighbor.

January

- ☐ Meet with your guidance counselor to review your course plan. Plot out your classes for junior year and senior year and include AP or IB courses as appropriate.

- ☐ January is National Mentor Month. If you have someone who mentored you, tell them *Thanks!*

- ☐ Keep saving for college idea: trade in gently used clothes for cash.

February

- ☐ It's not too early to think about summer plans. Do you want to work a part-time job? Many schools have websites that list job opportunities. If you are a talented athlete, consider attending a skills development camp.

- ☐ Celebrate Valentine's Day by mastering one *Social Scene Competency.*

☐ Volunteer idea: send letters to military personnel serving overseas.

March

☐ Celebrate spring by developing a *Sports and Fitness Competency*. Start training and feel great about being outside after the long winter!

☐ Invite a group of friends over to study and support each other to stay motivated. Even though spring is in the air, good grades are a primary consideration for college admission.

☐ Keep saving for college idea: start your own pet walking or doggy day care business.

April

☐ Spring break is a great time to volunteer on a mission trip. These trips are lots of fun and you benefit by gaining valuable leadership experience.

☐ Missed driver's education last year? Sign up now for summer classes.

☐ Read the *Calculate a Tip Competency* and then try out your new skill over dinner or a new haircut.

May

☐ Take SAT Subject and AP tests if needed.

☐ Celebrate Mother's Day with your mom, grandma or someone who has been like a mother to you.

☐ Keep saving for college idea: skip one coffee drink or fast food meal each week and put the savings in your college account.

June

☐ Celebrate your hard work and be proud all you've accomplished this year. Update your resume with recent GPA, awards, leadership and service hours.

☐ Take a practice ACT/SAT test. Consider taking a prep class or borrow a book from the library to study on your own.

☐ Celebrate Father's Day with your dad, grandpa or someone who has been a father figure to you.

☐ Unplug and read a book just for fun. Reading is a great way to relax and increases your vocabulary.

☐ Going on a summer vacation or just want to explore your own city? Choose two *Get Around Town Competencies* to master.

July

☐ Challenge yourself to try something new in nature: go tubing on a river, run a race for charity, visit a farm and pick your own produce.

☐ Visit a college and write down your impressions in the College Scorecard. Even though college students are not on campus, you can tour the school and connect with an admissions rep.

☐ Keep studying for ACT/SAT tests.

☐ Read from a variety of different sources including magazines, books, newspapers and the Internet.

☐ Keep saving for college idea: invite friends and family to a *Cook for College* BBQ.

August

☐ Make a list of three careers you think are interesting and then ask someone if you can shadow them for a day.

☐ Take another ACT/SAT practice test and compare your score to the one you took earlier this summer.

☐ Volunteer idea: lead a group at a day camp.

- ☐ Check to see if your fall classes have required summer reading assignments. If not, enjoy reading a book of your choice.

- ☐ Set your alarm clock back one week before school starts so your body clock can adjust to waking up early again.

My Milestone Map
Junior Year

Congratulations—you're half way to graduation! This is one of the most important years in your high school career so pay close attention to the timeline below.

September

- ☐ Make an appointment with your guidance counselor. Having a personal connection with your counselor will be helpful later when you need her to write a letter of recommendation for college applications.

- ☐ Find out when National Honor Society applications will be taken and how many hours of service are required for membership.

- ☐ Continue reviewing for the PSAT/ACT. Students who are familiar with the tests and practice the questions tend to receive higher test scores.

- ☐ Check out your school's website for information on the financial aid process.

- ☐ Keep saving for college idea: clean houses for neighborhood families.

October

- ☐ Meet with your guidance counselor. Find out what college related tools are on your school's website and if your school hosts college reps for in house visits.

- ☐ Register for the PSAT or PLAN and take the tests. A high score on the PSAT will qualify you for the National Merit Scholar competition.

- ☐ Attend a local college fair. Bring your college journal and make notes as you visit the individual booths.

- ☐ Junior year is extremely busy and balancing all your activities can put you on overload. Learn how to take care of yourself by exploring the *Stress Less Competency*.

- ☐ Volunteer idea: help out at a local animal shelter.

November

☐ Hit the books. Allow plenty of time for studying and don't be afraid to ask for help if you need it. Junior year grades are critical for next year's college applications.

☐ Continue to research colleges. Request information either online or via mail and you will also get your name in the college's database.

☐ Stay organized by creating a filing system to store college viewbooks, brochures, scholarship applications, and other information. You can purchase a bin and folders fairly inexpensively at a discount office store.

☐ Learn how to recognize the symptoms of depression and educate yourself on suicide prevention. Knowing how to help yourself or a friend could save a life!

☐ Keep saving for college idea: start your own snow shoveling business.

December

☐ PSAT results may arrive in your mailbox as early as December. Review your scores with your parents or counselor and make a study plan for the SAT/ACT tests.

- [ ] Register to take the SAT in January if you feel you are ready. Don't rush into taking this test as all scores are reported on your college score report. If you decide to take the test, find time over winter break to practice.

- [ ] Host a holiday party and ask friends to bring a gift to donate to a local shelter.

- [ ] De-stress over winter break. Watch a favorite movie, read, have a snowball fight with your friends, have a dance party, do a good deed for someone.

- [ ] Update your resume noting any new activities, special awards, leadership activities and volunteer hours.

January

- [ ] Review how many College Competencies® you have mastered and set a goal for the New Year.

- [ ] Take the SAT and ACT tests if you are well prepared.

- [ ] Meet with your guidance counselor to review your plan for senior year classes. Remember, colleges like to see students who continue to challenge themselves senior year.

- [ ] Plan a college visit for a long weekend in February or March.

☐ Keep saving for college idea: write a cover letter to use with summer job applications.

February

☐ Visit a college over President's Day holiday weekend. Journal your impressions in the College Scorecard while they're still fresh in your mind.

☐ Watch for SAT scores. Depending on your score, you may want to register to take the test again in April or May.

☐ Watch for AP exam registration information.

☐ Summer is only four months away! Consider taking a mission trip or attending a language camp. If you are a talented athlete, register for a showcase camp.

☐ Volunteer idea: serve dinner at a local soup kitchen.

March

☐ Continue to review for the SAT and ACT tests in April or May.

☐ Talk to your counselor about registering for SAT Subject tests in May and/or June.

☐ Spring break is a perfect time to fit in a few more college visits. If your chaperone is up to the challenge, ask to bring along a friend or two on the trip.

- ☐ Excelling in sports? Athletes should begin contacting college coaches. Alter your basic resume to create a separate resume for this purpose.
- ☐ Keep saving for college idea: start filling out applications for summer jobs.

April

- ☐ Take the ACT test.
- ☐ Plan out remaining visits to colleges on your list this spring, summer, and early fall. Call ahead to book appointments with busy admissions representatives.
- ☐ Learn how to use a spreadsheet program like Excel. This tool is very handy to help you compare college costs and track your scholarship activity.
- ☐ Have a conversation with your family about financing college. Start researching college costs and be sure to look beyond the published sticker price.
- ☐ Volunteer idea: celebrate Earth Day by organizing a litter walk.

May

- ☐ Take AP exams if you are taking AP classes.
- ☐ Take the SAT test.

☐ Volunteer idea: adopt a local park and plant flowers.

☐ May is prom season so review the *Health and Happiness and Social Scene Competencies* for recommendations on good decision making.

☐ Keep saving for college idea: organize a dog wash.

June

☐ Take the SAT test.

☐ You did it! Before you head off to the beach, take time to update your resume with latest GPA, new service hours, year-end awards, and special accomplishments.

☐ If you are a talented athlete, register with the NCAA Clearinghouse in early June to be a considered a *recruited* athlete.

☐ Read, read, read. Visit a local bookstore and ask them to recommend a title by a local author.

☐ Keep saving for college idea: plan a Parent's Night Out event.

July

☐ Check out the Common Application site to preview this year's essay questions. Pick one question and start writing.

- ☐ If you need to improve your SAT/ACT score, contact a private tutor.

- ☐ Do you know who your elected officials are? Develop this competency by contacting your local legislator about an issue you feel strongly about.

- ☐ Check to see if your fall classes have a summer reading assignment.

- ☐ Volunteer idea: help out at a 4th of July community celebration.

August

- ☐ Finish your Common App essay and ask for feedback. Did you answer the question being asked? Does this piece of writing describe the real you? Does it convey your strengths and special qualities?

- ☐ Make a list of teachers, counselors, coaches and other adults who have worked with you. Contact your top three and ask if they would be willing to write a letter of recommendation for your college applications and scholarships.

- ☐ Practice interviewing for upcoming college admissions appointments. Review the *World of Work Competencies* for tips on shaking hands and dressing your best.

☐ Find a hammock and reread a childhood favorite or finish your summer reading assignment.

☐ Keep saving for college idea: check your school's website for a list of scholarships.

My Milestone Map
Senior Year

Hang in there! You are almost to the finish line but there are still important milestones to complete. Giving your best effort now will pay off next year on campus!

September

☐ Meet with your guidance counselor to review your application plan. Offer him/her a copy of your resume to use as reference for letters of recommendation.

☐ Finalize your list of colleges and review application requirements. Check to see if any have early deadlines for merit scholarships.

My Milestone Map

- ☐ Request transcripts and teacher recommendations. Give teachers a copy of your resume so they have all your accomplishments at their fingertips.
- ☐ Finalize application essays.
- ☐ Schedule an overnight visit to your top choice school.

October

- ☐ Confirm applications have all the necessary pieces (application form, essay, letters from teachers and counselor, transcripts, ACT/SAT scores.) Requirements may differ by school so read the fine print.
- ☐ Submit applications and breathe a sigh of relief—the hardest part is done!
- ☐ Stay overnight at your top choice school during fall break.
- ☐ Take the ACT/SAT test if needed to improve your score.
- ☐ Keep saving for college idea: register with a reputable scholarship search site to identify potential awards.

November

- ☐ Confirm with each college admission office that all required documents have been received and your application is complete.

☐ Write thank you notes to those who wrote your letters of recommendation.

☐ Keep your grades up! Colleges check on senior performance and an increase in GPA can work in your favor for scholarships.

☐ If you are musically inclined, select audition numbers for music scholarships and start practicing.

☐ Have follow up discussion with your family on paying for college.

December

☐ Notify college admission offices of new accomplishments (improved grades, standard test scores, community awards).

☐ Create a spreadsheet to track the costs, scholarships, and important dates for each school you applied to.

☐ Take advantage of winter break to brush up on your cooking skills. Surprise your family by planning a meal, cooking it and cleaning up!

☐ Update your resume noting any new activities, special awards, leadership activities and volunteer hours.

☐ Keep saving for college idea: apply for scholarships.

January

☐ Ask your family to file their taxes as soon as possible since this info is required for the Free Application for Federal Student Aid (FAFSA.)

☐ Ask your family to complete the FAFSA.

☐ Notify colleges of new accomplishments (improved grades, standard test scores, community awards.)

☐ Schedule and/or attend musical audition.

☐ Volunteer idea: teach computer skills at a senior center.

February

☐ Check email frequently for notifications from colleges.

☐ Open your own checking account so you are equipped to pay for expenses during college. Learn how to manage your checkbook and balance your monthly statement.

☐ Review the *Make a Personal Appointment Competency*. It's good practice in case you need to make a dentist or doctor appointment while away at college.

☐ Volunteer idea: mentor a child.

☐ Keep saving for college idea: negotiate with your top schools.

March

- ☐ Compare awards and make visits to top choice schools to help you make your final selection.

- ☐ Keep your grades up—colleges check on senior performance.

- ☐ Master the *Be Careful with Credit Competency*. While it's convenient to have a credit card in college, it's very important to understand the fine print.

- ☐ Review the *Healthy Relationships and Just Say No Competencies* before heading out on spring break.

- ☐ Volunteer: tutor someone learning English as a second language.

April

- ☐ Watch for admission notifications.

- ☐ Send in your deposit to the college you've selected and notify colleges that you do not plan to attend. Deadline to notify colleges of your decision is usually May 1.

- ☐ Master the *Drunk Driver Safety Competency*. Protect yourself and others whether you are a passenger or behind the wheel.

- ☐ Volunteer: collect cans and take them to a recycling center.

☐ Celebrate Earth Day by making a new commitment to reduce what you buy, reuse something you have and recycle!

☐ Keep saving for college idea: apply early for summer jobs.

May

☐ Take AP exams if you are taking AP classes.

☐ Do you know how to use an ATM or a debit card? Read up on these two competencies in the *Show Me the Money* subject area to master these skills before leaving for college.

☐ Summer vacation is just around the corner! If you still have not learned how to do your own laundry, read the *Do Laundry Competency* and ask your family to give you instructions. Remember, hot water and red clothes equal pink laundry!

☐ Volunteer idea: make May Day baskets for a senior center.

June

☐ Celebrate your success at graduation!!!

☐ Send in your final transcript to the college you selected.

☐ Watch for information on freshman orientation and registration.

- ☐ Are there any College Competencies® you haven't mastered? Take advantage of free summer hours to finish learning these skills.

- ☐ Keep saving for college idea: deposit graduation money directly into your college account.

Recommended Reading for Parents

Don't Tell Me What To Do, Just Send Money: The Essential Guide to the College Parenting Years by Helen Johnson and Christine Schelhas-Miller (St. Martin's Press 2011)
This book helps parents lay the groundwork for a new kind of relationship so that they can help their child more effectively handle everything they'll encounter during their college years.

Letting Go: A Parent's Guide to Understanding the College Years by Karen Coburn and Madge Treeger (Harper Collins 2009)
Letting Go provides parents with valuable guidance on the emotional and social changes from the senior year in high school through college graduation. The newly updated version addresses topics including independence, identity and intimacy, safety and stress.

Queen Bees and Wanna Bees: Helping Your Daughter Survive Cliques, Gossip, Boyfriends, and the New Realities of Girl World by Rosalind Wiseman (Crown Publishing 2009)
Wiseman has revised and updated her groundbreaking book for a new generation of girls and explores how girls' experiences before

adolescence impact their teen years, future relationships, and overall success.

Raising Cain: Protecting the Emotional Life of Boys by Dan Kindlon, Ph.D., and Michael Thompson, Ph.D. (Random House 2000)

Two of the country's leading child psychologists share what they have learned in working with boys and their families. They identify the social and emotional challenges that boys encounter in school and show how parents can help boys cultivate emotional awareness and empathy—giving them the vital connections and support they need to navigate the social pressures of youth.

Surviving Your Adolescents: How to Manage and Let Go of Your 13-18 Year Olds by Thomas Phelan (Parent Magic 2012)

This book helps parents end hassles and improve their relationship with their adolescent. Parents learn how to communicate with teenagers, how to manage teenage risk-taking, how to let go in certain situations, and when to seek professional attention. Concise and encouraging, this resource walks parents through the ups and downs of parenting teenagers as their kids push towards independence.

***The Big Disconnect: Protecting Childhood and Family
Relationships in the Digital Age*** by Catherine Steiner-Adair Ed.D.
(Harper Collins 2013)

Psychologist Steiner-Adair explains how families are being
affected by chronic tech distractions. She offers advice on how to
develop a *sustainable family* and the importance of close,
significant interactions between parents and children.

The Complete Idiot's Guide to Financial Aid for College by
David Rye (Penguin Group 2008)

This comprehensive, fully updated edition shows readers how to
get scholarships, find the best financial aid packages for academic
or sports skills, improve one's chances of receiving financial aid,
take advantage of the new tax laws to build a college savings plan,
and much more.

The Financial Aid Handbook by Carol Stack and Ruth Vedvik
(Career Press 2011)

Searching for the right college at the right price? *The Financial Aid
Handbook* is an excellent resource that is written for students but
equally valuable for parents. It offers practical information

including a Best Bet list, tips on how to complete the FAFSA and more.

The Launching Years: Strategies for Parenting From Senior Year to College Life by Laura Kastner and Jennifer Wyatt (Clarkson Potter 2002)

Launching a child from home is second only to childbirth in its impact on a family. Parents can end up reeling with the empty nest blues, while teens find their powers of self-reliance stretched to the breaking point. *The Launching Years* is a trusted resource for keeping every member of the family sane.

The Sex-Wise Parent: The Parent's Guide to Protecting Your Child, Strengthening Your Family, and Talking to Kids About Sex, Abuse and Bullying by Janet Rosenzweig (Skyhorse 2012)

The Sex-Wise Parent will coach you to raise sexually safe and healthy sons and daughters. Discover the steps you can take to combine your own family's values with age-appropriate information for children at all stages of development.

You're On Your Own (But I'm Here If You Need Me):

Mentoring Your Child During the College Years by Marjorie

Savage (Fireside 2003)

This book helps parents identify the boundaries between necessary

involvement and respect for their child's independence and offers

advice on wide-ranging issues including teaching fiscal

responsibility and how to stay connected.

Friends Forever

Meet the Author

Beverly Gillen is the founder of Partners in Parenting Consulting and creator of the Top 100 College Competencies®. Drawing wisdom from the African proverb *it takes a village to raise a child*, Beverly uses her connections with community experts and resources to educate and encourage parents along their parenting journey.

Beverly has a B.S. in business management from the University of Minnesota, a parent educator license and experience as a birth and postpartum doula. Prior to founding Partners in Parenting Consulting, Beverly spent 27 years with a Fortune 500 company as a global commodity manager. She is a member of the Minnesota Association for College Admission Counseling and the Minnesota Council on Family Relations. She served on the Board of Directors for MyHealth teen clinic and volunteered as a Girl Scout leader for 15 years.

Beverly lives in Minnetonka, Minnesota with her husband, two daughters, and Australian Retriever. Her clients appreciate her empathic nature, playful teaching style and ability to listen and motivate positive change.

Check out our website for even more resources! *Take the Quiz* to see which College Competencies® you might want to develop. Visit *The Library* for new scholarship contests and reviews of the latest college prep resources. Meet our newest subject experts. Get inspired with our blog featuring the accomplishments of real life student leaders. Partners in Parenting Consulting is excited to be part of your team and we look forward to working together!

Partnersin **Parenting** Consulting

educate · empower · encourage

www.partnersinparentingconsulting.com

CPSIA information can be obtained at www.ICGtesting.com
Printed in the USA
LVOW04s1519280915

456036LV00015B/1043/P